THE TELESCOPE MAKERS

D1231546

THE TELESCOPE MAKERS

FROM GALILEO TO THE SPACE AGE

by

BARBARA LAND

ILLUSTRATED

THOMAS Y. CROWELL COMPANY

NEW YORK

PICTURE ACKNOWLEDGMENTS

Thanks are due the following for permission to reproduce the illustrations on the pages indicated: The American Museum of Natural History, 10, 24 (above), 30, 46–47, 129; Bell Laboratories, Inc., 190; The Bettmann Archive, 38, 50, 117, 153; California Institute of Technology, 138; Mount Wilson and Palomar Observatories, 24 (below), 78–79, 135, 141, 157, 161, 162, 186, 210, 227; National Aeronautics and Space Administration, 231; National Radio Astronomy Observatory, Green Bank, West Va., 189, 206; New York Public Library, Picture Collection, 8, 72, 82, 95, 100, 105, 134; New York Public Library, Prints Division, 33, 58, 62, 74; *The New York Times*, © 1933 by The New York Times Company, 193; The Royal Society of London, 121; United States Naval Research Laboratory, 210, 213, 218, 225; Dr. A. A. Wachmann, of the Hamburg Observatory, 165, 167, 183.

Copyright © 1968 by Barbara Land

Designed by Peter Landa

Manufactured in the United States of America

L.C. Card 68-21607

2 3 4 5 6 7 8 9 10

For Mike, Bob, and Jackie

ACKNOWLEDGMENTS

Some of the information in this book would have been un-available to me without the cooperation of scientists in-volved in the astronomy of the future, and some whose work has already made history. I am particularly grateful to Dr. A. A. Wachmann of the Hamburg Observatory, who graciously supplied facts, anecdotes, and pictures for the chapter on Bernhard Schmidt; to Dr. Herbert Friedman of the United States Naval Research Laboratory, who patiently answered my questions when he had a calendar full of other things to do; and to his helpful secretary, Miss Ruth Olson. For their capsule course in space astronomy, I thank Dr. Nancy Roman, director of the astronomy program at the National Aeronautics and Space Administration in Wash-ington, and Dr. James E. Kupperian, a space-age telescope maker, who is director of the astrophysics branch of NASA's Goddard Space Flight Center. I am equally grateful to Dr. Grote Reber, who carefully answered all my written queries as they followed him around the country, and who supplied some charming anecdotes during our brief conversations.

My special thanks to the people who arranged my meet-ings with the scientists: Nicholas Panagakos of the Goddard Institute for Space Studies, in New York; Richard Mittauer and Mike Harloff of NASA, in Washington; and Richard Baldwin and Miss Jennie Ewanoski of the Research Corpo-ration, in New York.

CONTENTS

Prologue   HANS LIPPERSHEY'S INGENIOUS   1
              SPYGLASS

Chapter 1   GALILEO'S NEW WINDOW ON   7
              THE HEAVENS

Chapter 2   JOHANNES KEPLER, THE   32
              NEARSIGHTED WIZARD

Chapter 3   ISAAC NEWTON'S REFLECTING   57
              TELESCOPE

Chapter 4   WILLIAM HERSCHEL'S GIANT   81
              REFLECTORS

Chapter 5   JOSEPH VON FRAUNHOFER'S   104
              LINES AND LENSES

Chapter 6   LORD ROSSE'S LEVIATHAN OF   120
              PARSONSTOWN

Chapter 7   GEORGE ELLERY HALE'S VIEW   137
              FROM PALOMAR

Chapter 8   BERNHARD SCHMIDT'S SKY CAMERA   164

Chapter 9   GROTE REBER'S LISTENING   188
                TELESCOPE

Chapter 10   HERBERT FRIEDMAN'S ROCKET   212
                TELESCOPES

Selected Bibliography   235

Index   239

HANS LIPPERSHEY'S INGENIOUS SPYGLASS

At first it was merely a toy—until an Italian mathematician made it a tool of science. A person could look through this slim metal tube and see distant objects as if they were close at hand—an amusing pastime.

The device had many names. The Dutch, who invented it, called it *kijkglas*. The French, who made it popular, called it *lunette d'approche*. The English named it *spyglass*, and Italians, at first, called it *occhiale*, the same name they used for spectacles. The mathematician Galileo, when he wrote about it in Latin, called it *perspiculum*. Only after he had shown the world what could be done with this tool did it find its permanent name—the *telescope*.

Before the invention found its way to Italy in 1609, it came to France from Holland. The king of France himself, Henry IV, had been the first man in Paris to own a spyglass, a gift to him from the government of the Netherlands. Whatever the king did and whatever he owned were usually copied as closely as possible by wealthy noblemen, so the spyglass became a coveted possession among his imitators. Dozens of orders poured into the little Dutch shop where the king's spyglass was made. The royal instrument had the name of its maker etched into the metal tube: *Hans Lippershey, Middelburg.*

Who was this Lippershey? Before the fame of his spyglass began to spread, he was simply a lens grinder, a maker of spectacles who owned a small shop in Middelburg, a flat, watery Dutch seaport that would have been swallowed up by the North Sea if the windmills had not kept pumping day and night to hold the water on the other side of the dikes. Lippershey's shop was one of several in Middelburg where citizens could have spectacles made.

Little is known about Lippershey's early years. He was born about 1570 in Wezel, Germany, and moved to Holland some time before 1600. He seems to have spent the rest of his life in Middelburg, where he was buried in 1619, just ten years after his spyglass made him famous.

Even though the facts about his life are scarce, there is one story that appears in almost every popular history of the telescope. Like the story of George Washington and the cherry tree, it has been disputed as fiction, but it has never been disproved. It could even be very close to the truth.

According to the story, Hans Lippershey was standing at the door of his shop one day polishing some lenses. He picked up two of the lenses and held them to the light to examine them for flaws. Both lenses were flat on one side, but on the other side, one was convex and one concave. Almost idly, he moved the convex lens in front of the concave one and looked through both at once. What he saw startled him so much that he almost dropped the lenses. A distant church tower seemed to jump to the door of the shop. He could even see the weathercock on top of the spire.

After toying with the lenses for a while, Lippershey had an idea for bringing more business into his shop. He mounted the lenses on a board in such a way that they could be moved back and forth to adjust the focus. Then, when customers came in for spectacles, he showed them the view of the church tower through the lenses. They marveled at the view, told their friends about it, and Lippershey became the most popular spectacle maker in town.

Meanwhile, Lippershey experimented with another set of lenses, enclosing them in opposite ends of a hollow tube. When he looked through the tube he was so pleased with the result that he decided to apply for a patent on his *kijkglas*, or "look glass."

Up to this point the story of Lippershey's invention may be merely a story, but what follows is a matter of record. On October 2, 1608, Lippershey sent one of his spyglasses as a gift to Mauritz of Nassau, the prince who was leading the Netherlands in a struggle for independence from Spain. The inventor requested a patent from the Estates General of the Netherlands. He asked for the exclusive right to manufacture such spyglasses for the next thirty years or an annual pension from the Dutch government. Four days later he received an official answer, refusing the patent "because too many people have knowledge of this invention."

There was a rumor that Lippershey's chief competitor in Middelburg, Zacharias Janssen, had made a spyglass as early as 1604. Travelers reported that similar instruments had been on sale in September at the Frankfurt Fair, about the time Lippershey was making his gift for the prince. On October 17 another Dutch lens grinder, Jacobus Metius of Alkmaar, applied for a patent on a viewing tube and was

refused for the same reason given Lippershey: too many
people knew about it.

No patent was granted, so the identity of the inventor of
the spyglass is still disputed by historians more than three
hundred and fifty years later. It is possible, of course, that all
these men discovered the principle of the spyglass independently. Perhaps the time was right; maybe astronomers were
ready for such an invention. Scholars in England and Germany, too, wrote about similar inventions at approximately
the same time.

Some historians trace the invention back to Italy, where
the first eyeglasses were made shortly before 1300. The earliest eyeglasses, called *occhiale*, were lenses set into a piece of
leather that could be attached to a cap. An Italian manuscript dated 1299 refers to them as "recently invented for
the benefit of old people whose eyesight has grown dull." A
tombstone dated 1317, in the Church of Mary Magdalen in
Florence, identifies Salvino degli Armati as *inventore degle
occhiale* ("inventor of eyeglasses").

Three hundred years after eyeglasses were invented, they
began to look more as they do today—lenses set into a metal
frame made to rest on the nose, with side pieces that hooked
behind the ears. This was still a long way from a telescope.

By 1604 lens grinding was a widespread skill. Spectacle
makers such as Lippershey and Janssen in Middelburg were
almost as plentiful as shoemakers. A Dutch encyclopedia
says that Janssen did make a spyglass in 1604, but that he
borrowed the idea from an Italian contemporary, Giambattista della Porta. The same encyclopedia accuses Hans Lippershey of trying to steal Janssen's idea and have it patented.
Other sources, such as *De Vero Telescopii Inventore* (The

True Inventor of the Telescope), published in the Hague in 1655, give the credit to Lippershey.

Whether or not Lippershey invented the spyglass, he deserves credit for making it known. If the Dutch government in 1608 knew about other manufacturers of spyglasses, they were impressed enough by the quality of Lippershey's instruments to order from him their official gift to the king of France. Prince Mauritz praised his *kijkglas* and suggested that he try to improve it so that it could be used for both eyes. Lippershey wasted no time in making the first binoculars on record and sent them to the prince. On December 13, 1608, the government ordered three more sets and paid the inventor 900 guilders.

By April 1609 there were copies of Lippershey's instruments for sale in Paris optical shops. At least one shop offered for sale, along with the spyglasses, a brochure written in French which suggested that the *lunette* might be used for "seeing stars which are not ordinarily in view because of their smallness." Most purchasers had other objectives in mind.

Military men soon discovered that spyglasses were useful for spotting enemy troops at a distance; ship captains used them to extend their vision at sea; French noblemen used them to watch pretty ladies as they drove by in open carriages. But nobody seems to have thought seriously of using the spyglass as a tool of science, until one French nobleman, Jacques Badovere, brought it to the attention of a friend in Italy. In the summer of 1609, Badovere wrote a letter to his former teacher of mathematics, Galileo Galilei of Padua. That letter touched off a series of events that made Lippershey's spyglass the most important tool of a new astronomy.

1

GALILEO'S NEW WINDOW ON THE HEAVENS

Galileo welcomed the letter from his former pupil with particular interest. It brought exciting news, he wrote later, confirming reports he had heard that "a certain Fleming had constructed a spyglass, by means of which visible objects, though very distant from the eye of the observer, were seen distinctly, as if near by."

At the time he received the letter, Galileo had never seen a spyglass, but he thought he might be able to make one. After asking a few questions about the Dutch instrument, he began reading books about light—particularly the way it bends when it passes through glass. Then he set out to construct his own spyglass. Ten months later, he completed a small instrument, perhaps two feet long, and wrote down exactly what he had done:

I prepared a tube, at first of lead, in the ends of which I fitted two glass lenses, both plane on one side, but on the other side one spherically convex and the other concave. Then, bringing to my eye the concave lens, I saw objects satisfactorily large and near, for they appeared one-third of the distance off and nine times larger than when they are seen with the natural eye alone. I

7

Galileo Galilei (1564–1642).

shortly thereafter constructed another tube with more nicety, which magnified objects more than sixty times. At length, by sparing neither labor nor expense, I succeeded in constructing for myself an instrument so superior that objects seen through it appear magnified nearly a thousand times, and more than thirty times nearer than if viewed by the natural powers of sight alone.

With this instrument the mathematician Galileo watched the twilight sky on January 11, 1610, waiting for the appearance of Jupiter, the evening star. Four days earlier, on January 7, his curiosity had been aroused by three small stars—at least he assumed they were stars—that seemed in his telescope to lie in a straight line with Jupiter, two to the east and one to the west of the planet. The following night, to his surprise, he saw all three small stars to the west of Jupiter.

Was Jupiter moving eastward, instead of westward as the astronomers calculated? Galileo didn't know what to make of the phenomenon, but he was determined to find out what it meant. The next night, January 9, was too cloudy for observations, but on the tenth Jupiter appeared with only *two* of its small companions. Galileo began to suspect that these tiny stars were not stars at all. Were they moons, encircling Jupiter as our own moon circled earth?

Each night as he watched the sky he wrote down his observations and made little drawings of the positions of Jupiter's companions.

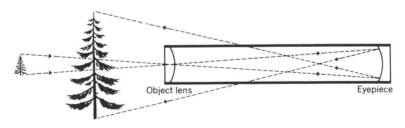

Galileo's Telescope

Night after night, Galileo watched and recorded his observations of Jupiter's small satellites.

Now, on January 11, Galileo raised his spyglass and saw that one of the starlets was twice its former size. Did this mean it had moved closer to the observer?

I had now decided beyond all question [he wrote later] that there existed in the heavens three stars wandering about Jupiter as do Venus and Mercury about the sun, and this became plainer than daylight from observations on similar occasions which followed. Nor were there just three such stars: four wanderers complete their revolutions about Jupiter, and of their alterations as observed more precisely later on we shall give a description here. Also I measured the distances between them by means of the spyglass . . . . Moreover, I recorded the times of the observations, especially when more than one was made during the same night—for the revolutions of these planets are so speedily completed that it is usually possible to take even their hourly variations.

Holding the spyglass to his eye, Galileo felt he was holding the key to a radical new truth. His careful measurements and records were being assembled for a purpose. Perhaps now he would be able to prove what he had believed secretly for a long time—that the earth was not the center of all creation, but a planet like the others that traveled around the sun.

The idea was not his alone. A Polish astronomer and canon of the Church, Nicolaus Copernicus, who died twenty-one years before Galileo was born, had suggested a sun-centered universe. His book, *On the Revolutions of the Heavenly Spheres*, published in 1543, was so hard to read that few nonmathematicians had even tried. But Galileo, who was a mathematician, found it fascinating.

The Church simply ignored Copernicus and continued to teach that the earth was the center of the universe. Although the Church frowned on teachers who departed from official doctrine, Galileo believed it would change its teachings if he could present convincing evidence to support Copernicus. Now, with the spyglass, he could *show* people the truth. The theologians need only look at the sky to see for themselves.

As simply and clearly as he could, Galileo set down a detailed report of what he had discovered. The report was published in March 1610 in a pamphlet called *Siderius Nuncius*. The Latin title has been translated as *Message from the Stars*, *The Sidereal Messenger*, *Messenger from the Stars*, and most often, *The Starry Messenger*. When Galileo was criticized by a churchman for calling himself the messenger of Heaven, he replied that *nuncius* means "message" as well as "messenger." Scholars still disagree about the translation.

Galileo wrote his report in Latin, then the international language of scholars, because he wanted all of Europe's astronomers and philosophers to know what he had seen. He suspected that his findings would cause a revolution in the way these scholars—and all men—thought about the universe, the earth, and themselves.

On the title page of his booklet Galileo summed up, in a wordy subtitle which is reproduced on the opposite page, all the wonders the reader would find inside:

Revealing great, unusual, and remarkable
spectacles, opening these to the
consideration of every man,
and especially of

PHILOSOPHERS and ASTRONOMERS

As observed by

GALILEO GALILEI
Gentleman of Florence

Professor of Mathematics in the
University of Padua

With the aid of a
SPYGLASS
lately invented by him

On the FACE OF THE MOON, IN INNUMERABLE FIXED STARS,
in NEBULAE

and above all in
FOUR PLANETS
swiftly revolving about Jupiter at differing distances
and periods, and known to no one before the author
recently perceived them and decided to name them
THE MEDICEAN STARS

Venice 1610

"The Medicean Stars" were four of Jupiter's twelve moons, the first ones discovered and the only ones known for nearly three hundred years afterward. Galileo named them in honor of Cosimo de' Medici, Grand Duke of Tuscany, hoping to gain favor with the powerful and wealthy Medici family of Florence, the Tuscan capital. He had once tutored the young duke in mathematics. Now, perhaps, the family could give him a teaching appointment in Florence. After seventeen years at Padua, in the Republic of Venice, Galileo was impatient to return to his native Tuscany.

Galileo loved Florence and felt that it was his true home, though he had been born fifty miles away in Pisa. His father, Vincenzo Galilei, had come from an ancient Florentine family. His ancestors had taken part in the artistic and intellectual life of the city during the Renaissance, when men such as Leonardo da Vinci, Dante, and Michelangelo had made Florence a center of art and ideas. Vincenzo Galilei had a variety of talents and interests, including music and mathematics. Some of his words on musical theory are still preserved in the Central National Library of Florence.

In Vincenzo's time the family fortune had declined, and he had to make a living, so he became a cloth merchant. Florence was a center for textile weaving, but Pisa was a better center for trading, so Vincenzo moved to Pisa. There he married Julia Ammanati in 1562 and there their first child, Galileo, was born on February 15, 1564. He was named for a distinguished ancestor, a doctor and magistrate named Galileo, in whose honor the rest of the family had changed its name from Bonajuti to Galilei. When the

magistrate's namesake was ten years old, the family returned to Florence.

The young Galileo grew up in an exciting age of exploration and conquest. Columbus had discovered the New
World just seventy-two years before his birth. While Galileo was growing up in Italy, William Shakespeare, just two
months younger, was beginning to scribble verses in an
English village. During Galileo's lifetime the first American
colonies were founded by Spanish, French, and English set-
tlers; Portuguese seamen discovered still another continent,
Australia. Fighting for Queen Elizabeth of England, Sir
Francis Drake led the British fleet to victory over the "in-
vincible" Spanish Armada. In 1581, when Galileo was
seventeen, Pope Gregory XIII received in Rome two am-
bassadors from remote Japan. The world was getting
smaller all the time.

That year, 1581, was an important one in Galileo's life.
His boyhood was behind him and he had to settle down to
the serious business of preparing for a career. His elemen-
tary education had been like that of most Florentine boys
of his class—Latin and Greek with tutors and a course in
logic with monks at the monastery of Santa Maria di
Vallombrossa, near Florence. His father had taught him to
play the lute and the organ, and he dabbled in sketching
and painting.

In the fall of 1581 Galileo returned to Pisa to enter the
university as a student of medicine. Not that he particularly
wanted to be a doctor. At that time he was far more interested in painting and music, but his father urged him to
study medicine and be assured of making a living. Galileo
would have to support himself somehow, Vincenzo argued,

and he showed no enthusiasm at all for his father's cloth business.

Galileo pursued his studies in medicine for at least three years, but he never became a doctor. During his third year at the University of Pisa he discovered mathematics and became so fascinated by numbers that he abandoned medicine altogether. Today it may seem incredible that a nineteen-year-old boy could have reached the university stage in his education without having studied mathematics, but in Galileo's day it was not considered necessary for a doctor to know much more than simple arithmetic. In 1583, however, Galileo met Ostilio Ricci, court mathematician of the grand duke of Tuscany.

According to the custom of Renaissance nobility, the grand duke had taken into his court at Florence about sixty young pages from noble European families, whom he was educating with the best teachers available. Ostilio Ricci, a friend of Galileo's father, was reputedly the best teacher of mathematics in Italy. Ricci often visited Pisa with the grand duke, and on one of his visits he was invited to lecture on the geometry of Euclid. Vincenzo Galilei wrote to his son and advised him to go and hear Ricci. Galileo went, listened, and made up his mind to hear more.

Some historians have said that Vincenzo tried to discourage Galileo's interest in mathematics, to persuade him to concentrate only on medicine. Galileo's own son has told the story quite differently. After Galileo's death he wrote:

Galileo, occupied in the study of medicine, for some time showed himself disinclined to mathematics, although his father, who was highly proficient in it, exhorted him to study it. Finally, to satisfy his father he applied his mind to it, but no sooner did he begin to taste the manner of demonstrating and the way of reaching the knowledge of truth, than, abandoning any other studies, he gave himself entirely to mathematics.

With his father's approval Galileo arranged to be tutored by Ricci. As the court mathematician taught him the fundamental mathematical principles, Galileo began to apply them to things he saw happening around him. Mathematics, he discovered, could be a tool to help him answer some of the hundreds of questions that prodded him eternally to ask more questions—especially about the way things move.

Why, for example, did a lamp swinging from the ceiling in the cathedral of Pisa follow the particular rhythmic pattern he noticed as he tried to time it with his pulse? His musical training made him almost instinctively count the beats. Back and forth, back and forth—the swing of the lamp kept up a steady tempo, even as the path of each swing became shorter and shorter.

Common sense led him to expect the lamp to slow down as it swung through smaller and smaller distances. But when he counted the beats of his pulse, as he had been taught to do in medical school, he found that each swing lasted the same number of beats, from the first long arcs to the final short ones.

This observation stirred his curiosity enough to make him wonder about it after he left the cathedral. In the home of the relatives with whom he lived while studying at Pisa, Galileo set up a series of experiments to prove to himself that the swinging lamp obeyed a natural law that would apply to all swinging objects. As he described his procedure:

I took two balls, one of lead and one of cork, the former more than a hundred times heavier than the latter, and suspended them by means of two equally fine threads, each four or five cubits long. Pulling each ball aside from the perpendicular, I let them go at the same instant. They, falling along the circumferences of circles having these equal strings for semi-diameters, passed beyond the perpendicular and returned along the same path. These free goings and returnings, repeated a hundred times, showed clearly that the heavy body maintains so nearly the period of the light body that neither in a hundred swings, nor even in a thousand, will the former anticipate the latter by as much as a single moment, so perfectly do they keep step.

Galileo had discovered a fundamental law of physics, the law of *isochronism*—or equal times—for objects swinging through equal arcs. The weight of the objects didn't matter as long as they were fastened to strings or chains or handles of equal length.

The method Galileo described so carefully is familiar to every modern scientist. He *observed* natural happenings, guessed at a law they might illustrate, set up *experiments*, repeating them over and over and carefully recording the results; then he drew *conclusions*.

The method was not entirely new. The Greeks had performed experiments, such as Archimedes' famous test of the behavior of bodies immersed in water. Medieval scientists had experimented in optics and magnetism, but Galileo was one of the first, if not the first, to use the experimental method in the study of motion. He set an example that became the foundation for modern science; he became the first modern physicist.

Young Galileo was pleased with what he had discovered and eager to tell his professors about it. If he expected approval, he was disappointed. They thought of him as an arrogant, presumptuous young man who talked too much, and they were not inclined to listen. He found the atmosphere at Pisa increasingly unfriendly. Finally he decided it was pointless to go on with his studies there.

In 1586, without a degree from the university, Galileo returned to Florence and his father's house to continue his studies alone. He read Euclid and Archimedes and wrote a few pamphlets. To make money he did tutoring and a little lecturing on literature and mathematics, but he was not making a living. His father was getting old and the family needed financial help from its eldest son.

Determined to find a permanent teaching post, Galileo called on his father's influential friends and asked for help. One of these friends, a mathematically inclined nobleman named Guidobaldo del Monte, recommended him to the University of Pisa as a lecturer. After his uncomfortable experiences as a student at Pisa, Galileo was not enthusiastic about the idea, but he had to have a paying job. When the position was offered he accepted it.

Galileo was twenty-five in 1589 when he moved back to Pisa to begin lecturing in mathematics at the university. The salary was small, but it paid his living expenses and allowed him enough time to continue with his studies.

He stayed only three years, but during this time he wrote a book in Latin, *De Motu* (On Motion), which attempted to disprove some of Aristotle's ideas. One of the most revolutionary statements in the book contradicted Aristotle's notion that falling bodies of the same material but of different weights will travel at speeds proportional to their weights. In other words, according to Aristotle, if two objects traveled the same distance, the heavier one would hit the ground first. Galileo denied this. He concluded that two bodies of the same substance, no matter what the difference in their weights, would fall the same distance in the same time.

A popular story describes Galileo's dramatic demonstration of this principle. One day, so the story goes, a crowd of students and teachers assembled at the base of the Leaning Tower of Pisa to watch him drop two lead balls, one much heavier than the other, from the top of the tower. Since the balls reached the ground at the same time, Galileo had proved Aristotle wrong.

Later historians doubted the truth of this story when they discovered that the same experiment had been recorded as performed in Holland by a Dutch mathematician, Simon Stevinus, who lived from 1548 to 1620. Besides, Galileo did not tell the story himself, and he was never inclined to be modest about his successes. The Tower of Pisa story is told in the earliest biography of Galileo, written by Vincenzo Viviani, a worshipful pupil who knew him in his old age and was inclined to embroider the details of stories he told about his master.

Whether or not Galileo dropped the weights from the Leaning Tower, he did write down his conclusions about falling bodies in *De Motu*. Designed as a textbook, *De Motu* was not published during Galileo's life, but copies of the manuscript were passed around at the time.

The manuscript did nothing to increase Galileo's popularity with his colleagues. Those who remembered him as a conceited student found him even more irritatingly self-assured and sarcastic as a lecturer. His arrogant contradiction of Aristotle's teachings made people uncomfortable. If he felt ill at ease among them he was determined not to show it, but equally determined to find another job as soon as possible.

He had other reasons for wanting to leave Pisa. His father was ill in Florence and his mother, brother, and two unmarried sisters turned to Galileo for financial help. The miserable salary at Pisa was barely enough to support one man, so Galileo applied to the University of Padua, in the Republic of Venice, where he knew there was an opening for a professor of mathematics. But a year went by and no appointment was made.

About this time, one of Galileo's sisters was to be married. According to the custom of the day she had to have a dowry—a certain amount of money or property to contribute to the marriage. Galileo had promised her a dowry and somehow he managed to save enough from his earnings to provide one. It had been a struggle and he knew he had to have more money—quickly. Again he applied to Padua. There was no reply.

Soon after his sister's wedding, their father died and Galileo was desperate. Now the rest of the family depended wholly on him. Taking a last-chance gamble, he traveled to Venice and offered his services to the Republic.

Whatever he may have expected to find in Venice, even an optimist like Galileo must have been surprised at the reception he received. After the hostility that surrounded him in Pisa, he could hardly have been prepared for the openhearted welcome he found in the gay city of canals. Noble families opened the doors of their glittering palaces to him, laughed at his wit, complimented his charm, and showered him with invitations. Then came the announcement he had hoped for. He was appointed to the coveted chair of mathematics at the University of Padua. His family problems were solved—for the moment.

Galileo spent eighteen years in Padua, the most creative years of his life. In the free atmosphere of the Venetian republic he could say whatever he pleased without fear of losing his job. His lectures became so popular that the classrooms overflowed and he had to speak in the open air. Some of his pupils boarded with him in the spacious house where he set up a workshop and—after he made his famous spyglass—an outdoor observatory. The house still stands, a massive red stone building, now numbered 31 Via Galileo Galilei.

In Padua Galileo made most of the studies in mechanics that became the foundation of modern physics. There he constructed the first telescope to be used exclusively for studying the stars. There, from his courtyard observatory, he first saw the moons of Jupiter, the countless stars of the Milky Way, and the rugged craters of the moon.

For centuries before Galileo, men had found in the sky only what their eyes could see—the same sun, stars, and planets; an occasional comet or nova, and always the smooth, shining moon. Now in 1609, "with the aid of a spyglass lately invented," Galileo saw things no other man had seen.

The moon, he discovered, was not as people thought it was.

I have been led to the opinion and conviction [he wrote in *Message from the Stars*] that the surface of the moon is not smooth, uniform, and precisely spherical as a great number of philosophers believe it to be, but is uneven, rough, and full of cavities and prominences, being not unlike the face of the earth, relieved by chains of mountains and deep valleys. The things I have seen by which I was enabled to draw this conclusion are as follows. . . .

In careful detail Galileo described what he had seen, night after night, as he watched the moon wax from new to full, wane, and reappear as another new moon. He illustrated his account with drawings of a lunar surface that looks remarkably like the moonscape shown in later astronomical photographs.

His straightforward scientific style occasionally becomes quite vivid. One section of the moon, he says:

where it is spotted as the tail of a peacock is sprinkled with azure eyes, resembles those glass vases which have been plunged while still hot into cold water and have thus acquired a crackled and wavy surface, from which they receive their common name of "ice cups."

After making these discoveries about the moon, Galileo turned his spyglass to the stars. He was the first to notice that planets seen through a telescope look different from stars.

The planets [he wrote] show their globes perfectly round and definitely bounded, looking like little moons, spherical and flooded all over with light. The fixed stars are never seen to be bounded by a circular periphery, but have rather the aspect of blazes whose rays vibrate about them and scintillate a great deal. Viewed with a spyglass they appear of a shape similar to that which they present to the naked eye, but sufficiently enlarged so that a star of the fifth or sixth magnitude seems equal to the Dog Star, largest of all the fixed stars.

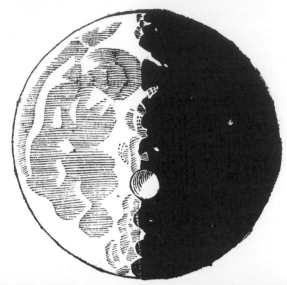

Galileo's drawing of the moon shows craters similar to those revealed three hundred years later by the Mount Wilson telescope.

In writing about the Milky Way, Galileo said that it is in fact nothing but a congress of innumerable stars grouped together in clusters. Upon whatever part of it the spyglass is directed, a vast crowd of stars is immediately presented to view. Many of them are rather large and quite bright, while the number of smaller ones is quite beyond calculation.

After revealing these "remarkable spectacles," Galileo was ready to unveil his prize discovery:

There remains the matter which in my opinion deserves to be considered the most important of all—the disclosure of four PLANETS never seen from the creation of the world up to our own time.

And he described in detail the events leading up to his discovery of the moons of Jupiter.

The publication of *Message from the Stars* made the author a celebrity as far away as Germany and England. The Venetian republic showered Galileo with attention. The University of Padua raised his salary to 1,000 florins a year and gave him his job for life. He was invited to Rome to meet princes, cardinals, and even Pope Paul V, who granted very few audiences.

Galileo was especially pleased at an invitation to become the sixth member of the recently founded Accademia del Lincei (Academy of the Lynxes). It was the first society in the world devoted exclusively to the advancement of science and philosophy, forerunner of such groups as the Royal Society of London and Benjamin Franklin's Philosophical Society in Philadelphia.

On April 14, 1611, the founder of the Lincean Academy, Prince Federico Cesi, gave a banquet in his Roman villa. He invited nobles and scholars to meet Galileo. The date became significant in the history of astronomy. That night Galileo's spyglass received a new name—*telescope*. The word was coined by a charter member of the Lincean Academy, the mathematician Ionnes Demisiani, who combined two Greek words meaning "far" and "to look" to describe Galileo's far-looking instrument. Galileo had called it *occhiale* in Italian and *perspiculum* in Latin, but Demisiani's *telescopio* was the name that became permanent.

At the banquet Prince Cesi introduced Galileo and invited his guests to examine his telescope, a long, slim tube covered in gold-tooled red leather. Then they all trooped outside to look at the moon. Through the telescope Cesi's friends saw for themselves the moon's astonishing craters.

Other gatherings were less successful. Galileo was puzzled and angry when a few skeptical scholars refused to look into the telescope at all. In the universities rigid followers of Aristotle refused to believe in Jupiter's moons simply because Aristotle had never said anything about them. One critic suggested that Galileo must have put "small bodies" inside his telescope to deceive people.

Many theologians refused to believe Galileo's statements because they were "incompatible with the doctrines of the Holy Scriptures." In the Florentine Church of Santa Maria Novella a Dominican priest delivered a rousing sermon denouncing mathematics as the art of the devil. Mathematicians, he said, should be expelled from all Christian lands as heretics.

At about this time Galileo was surprised to learn that formal charges had been brought against him to the Inquisition, the high tribunal of the Roman Church. No action was taken against him right away, but he was baffled. He did not feel that he had harmed the Church by simply reporting what he had seen. He had many good friends in the Church, including Cardinal Barberini, who later became Pope. The Cardinal advised Galileo to believe what he pleased, but to keep quiet in public.

In 1615 the Church took official notice of the source of Galileo's alleged heresy: *On the Revolutions of the Heavenly Spheres* by Copernicus. The book had been approved seventy-two years earlier by the Pope to whom it was dedicated, Leo X. Now it was placed on the Church's *Index* of forbidden books. Galileo was asked to stop teaching heresy, no matter what he saw through his telescope.

He tried to comply with this request, but began to feel more and more stifled. Then suddenly there was hope of freedom. In 1623 his friend Maffeo, Cardinal Barberini, became Pope Urban VIII. Perhaps he would lift some of the restrictions limiting Galileo's work.

A year later, as soon as he could travel to Rome, Galileo visited his friend at the Vatican. They talked for a long time and the Pope agreed—or Galileo *thought* he agreed— that Galileo should be allowed to write about the Copernican system, as long as he treated it as a mere hypothesis, not accepted truth. Convinced that he could present his views without antagonizing the Church, Galileo set to work on a defense of the Copernican system.

In 1632, when Galileo published his *Dialogue of the Two Greatest Systems of the World*, the Church gave the book its *imprimatur*, or stamp of approval. Galileo had reason to believe that his troubles were over. He was wrong.

Without warning the *Dialogue* was suppressed just a few

months after its publication. From Rome the publisher received an order not to sell any more copies. Soon afterward Galileo was called to Rome to appear before the tribunal of the Inquisition.

He was stunned. What had he done to offend the Church? He had submitted the manuscript for approval and had made all the changes suggested by the authorities. The book had been licensed for publication in Rome and in Florence. Now the Church had withdrawn the license. What had gone wrong?

Galileo was never able to understand exactly why the Church suddenly reversed its position. Even now, more than three hundred years later, historians can only speculate. One thing was clear—Pope Urban VIII was angry. Galileo's friend had become his enemy. Many historians believe that the Pope considered Galileo's book a personal insult, that he felt Galileo was making fun of him. If Galileo did insult the Pope, it was probably not intentional. He had always shown the greatest respect for his friend. But a look at the *Dialogue* shows why the Pope may have been offended.

The *Dialogue* is simply a conversation among three men discussing two theories of the universe—the Ptolemaic, earth-centered system defended by the Church and the Copernican, sun-centered system supported by Galileo. The title page states very carefully that "the philosophical and natural reasons for both are advanced inconclusively." Galileo was trying to be impartial. As the Pope had advised, he was presenting his ideas as hypotheses, not facts.

Unfortunately the *Dialogue* as a whole did not seem at all impartial. Maybe Galileo didn't realize how obvious it seemed to his critics, but there was no mistaking the author's opinion as to which view was the true one.

What probably offended the Pope most of all was the presentation of the three men discussing the two systems. Galileo called them Sagredo, Salviati, and Simplicio. The first two were named after good friends of Galileo's who had died. Salviati represented the scientist who supported the Copernican doctrine held by Galileo. Sagredo, the educated layman and philosopher, tried to weigh both sides. Simplicio, the "simple-minded," was an old-fashioned Aristotelian who refused to listen to any argument not found in accepted texts. Simplicio voiced the opinions of the Church, whose official spokesman was the Pope. Was Galileo calling the Pope "simple-minded"?

For reasons he never fully understood, Galileo found himself the enemy of the Church. On June 22, 1633, he was taken to a monastery in the center of Rome, made to kneel before the tribunal of the Inquisition, and forced to deny his belief in the sun-centered system. His works were placed on the *Index* and he was put under house arrest. The Church allowed him to go back to his villa in Arcetri, near Florence, but he was watched constantly and allowed to leave Arcetri only twice during the rest of his life.

Galileo, now old and feeble and almost blind, never stopped working. Even as a prisoner in his seventies he managed to write one more book—some say his greatest work—*Demonstrations Concerning Two New Sciences*. The manuscript of this book that launched modern physics was smuggled to Holland by one of Galileo's Venetian friends and was published there in 1638. Galileo pretended that he didn't know how it had found its way to Holland.

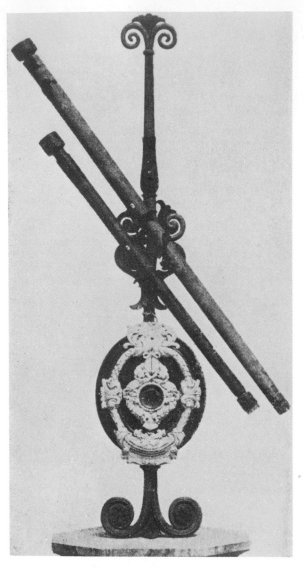

Two of Galileo's telescopes are preserved in a Florence museum. The ivory frame holds a broken lens from the telescope used by Galileo when he discovered four of Jupiter's moons.

When Galileo was seventy-eight, while working on an analysis of the force of percussion, he was stricken by a fever. After two months of illness he died on January 8, 1642. His beloved city, Florence, voted to erect a monument to him in the Church of Santa Croce, but Pope Urban forbade it. A heretic could not be buried in the resting place of great Florentines. For almost a hundred years Galileo's body lay in the basement of the church. Finally, in 1737, Pope Clement XII approved the monument that stands in the church today.

Visitors to Florence still flock to Santa Croce to see Galileo's monument. They also crowd into the Museum of the History of Science to see another monument to his genius. There, mounted on an ornate metal stand, are two of his telescopes—Galileo's keys to the new astronomy.

2

JOHANNES KEPLER,
THE NEARSIGHTED WIZARD

Even before Galileo built his famous telescopes, another star gazer who supported Copernicus was thinking and writing about the possibility of using lenses to bring the stars closer.

Johannes Kepler, a German mathematician, was one of Galileo's most enthusiastic admirers. The two men had corresponded as early as 1597, after Kepler wrote *The Cosmic Mystery*, a book defending the Copernican system. Galileo had praised him as "an associate in the study of truth who is a friend of truth." Kepler tried to keep the correspondence going, but when Galileo didn't answer his letters he finally stopped writing.

In 1610, when Kepler heard about Galileo's discoveries with his spyglass, he was ready with a set of mathematical proofs that made the study of optics forever a part of astronomy.

Galileo had made the telescope a tool of science, but his chief interest was in *what* the telescope revealed rather than in *how* and *why* it worked. Kepler, who could never trust

Johannes Kepler (1571–1630).

his own observations because of his extremely poor eyesight, was far more interested in the why and how.

As a child Kepler had suffered from multiple vision (seeing two or four images instead of one). As he grew older this condition improved but he became increasingly nearsighted. His studies of the stars led him to become interested in lenses and how they could help him see. As early as

1600 he made himself a pair of concave spectacles for star gazing and experimented with various combinations of lenses. There was nothing new about spectacles in Kepler's time, but the nearsighted astronomer wanted to know how they worked—why certain lenses made it possible for his eye to see what it could not see unaided.

Kepler read everything he could find about optics—which was precious little in 1600. The most modern textbook he could find was written around 1270 by a Polish scholar named Vitellio. Kepler decided to revise Vitellio, going back to Greek and Arabic sources, exploring unanswered questions, adding discoveries of his own. This revised text, called A *Supplement to Vitellio*, was published in 1604. It attracted little attention then, but after Galileo introduced the telescope to astronomers, they began to study Kepler's book with greater interest.

They were astounded at his foresight. Even in 1604 Kepler had anticipated many problems that existed for astronomers only after the introduction of the telescope six years later. Chief among these was the problem of refraction—the bending of light when it passes from one medium into another.

When light remains within any one medium—whether it is air, water, glass, or a vacuum—the beam does not bend; it travels in a straight line. But whenever the light passes from one medium to another, it bends. When, for example, a beam of light passes from air into glass or water, it changes direction if it strikes the surface of the new medium at any angle other than the perpendicular. In other words: at noon in the tropics, if the sun is exactly overhead, a beam of sunlight will pass through the surface of a pond without bending, because it is traveling in a line perpendicular to the surface of the pond. But at four o'clock, when the sun is nearer the horizon, the beam of sunlight strikes the surface of the pond at an angle and bends sharply.

In Kepler's time, nobody could explain why this happens. Kepler wanted to find a mathematical law of refraction that would describe exactly how much a beam of light bends when it passes through a lens, or from air into water. Kepler never found his law of refraction, but in searching for it he asked and answered questions that led other scientists to a formula, an indispensable tool in the science of optics.

In *A Supplement to Vitellio,* later known as Kepler's *Optics,* the mathematician also introduced for the first time the principle of photomeasurement—that *the intensity of light diminishes with the square of the distance from the source.* This principle is still taught in modern physics and astronomy classes.

Kepler's work had been published six years before he heard about Galileo's discovery of the moons of Jupiter with his spyglass. At that time Kepler was living in Prague as Imperial Mathematician at the court of Rudolph II, Emperor of the Holy Roman Empire. At thirty nine, he was recognized as far away as the British Isles as one of the world's foremost astronomers and mathematicians.

On April 8, 1610, Kepler was visited by the Tuscan ambassador Julian de' Medici, who brought him a gift from Galileo—a copy of *Message from the Stars.* Kepler had already borrowed the emperor's copy, received from Galileo a few days earlier, but he was delighted to have his own. He was especially pleased when de' Medici told him that Galileo had asked for Kepler's opinion of his work. The German mathematician replied that he would be honored to correspond with Galileo again.

With genuine enthusiasm he devoted the next few days to writing an open letter to Galileo, later published as *Conversation with the Star Messenger*.

The letter overflowed with praise for Galileo, with promises to support him "in the battle against reactionaries who reject everything that is unknown as unbelievable, and regard everything that departs from Aristotle as a desecration."

With a sudden foresight, Kepler speculated: "Perhaps I shall be considered reckless because I accept your claims as true without being able to add my own observations. But how could I distrust a reliable mathematician whose art of language alone demonstrates the straightness of his judgment?"

After covering eight pages with questions, theories, and proposals for future work, Kepler made a careful copy of the letter and gave it to a courier who was to leave for Italy on April 19. When the letter reached Padua, Galileo wasted no time in making use of it. This letter from the Imperial Mathematician was exactly the kind of ammunition he needed to strike back at his Italian critics. He boasted about the letter, but he didn't answer it—or send any message of thanks to Johannes Kepler.

Meanwhile, Kepler found himself criticized for giving such trusting support to something he had not seen for himself. He received letters from prominent Italians, who denied that Galileo's "Medicean planets" could be seen through any spyglass.

Disturbed by his inability to find anyone who would

testify to having seen what Galileo claimed to have seen, Kepler wrote and asked to borrow Galileo's telescope, "so that at last I too can enjoy, like yourself, the spectacle of the skies." He asked also for the names of some witnesses, since he was unable to name any testimony except Galileo's.

This time he received an answer, dated August 19. Addressing him as "My most learned Kepler," Galileo wrote:

"I wish to thank you for being the first, and almost the only person who completely accepted my assertions—though you had no proof—thanks to your frank and noble mind." Galileo regretted that he could not lend Kepler his telescope because he had given it to the grand duke. But he promised that he would be making more telescopes. Kepler never received one, though he heard of various noblemen who did receive them as gifts from Galileo.

By the time Galileo's letter reached Prague, Kepler had already borrowed a telescope, Galileo's gift to the duke of Bavaria, and had seen for himself the moons of Jupiter. In September 1610 he wrote a pamphlet, *Observation Report of Jupiter's Four Wandering Satellites*, confirming Galileo's discoveries. It was the first published support of Galileo by another observer of Jupiter's moons. It was also the first time the word "satellite," coined by Kepler, appeared in print.

As soon as he had seen for himself through the duke's telescope how lenses could open up the sky, Kepler began thinking of ways to improve Galileo's instrument. Galileo's combination of lenses—one plano-concave and one plano-convex—made a distant star seem many times closer and larger. But remarkable as it was, this telescope covered a

Astronomers of Kepler's time used large quadrants to study the stars until Galileo introduced the telescope as a better tool.

very narrow field and was not easy to focus. Kepler suggested using two double convex lenses of different sizes. The arrangement he proposed would provide a brighter image and a much wider field of vision. The image would be upside down, but astronomers didn't mind that.

Kepler described his improved telescope in a book he called *Dioptrice*, dedicated to the duke of Bavaria and published in 1610. The simple book contained 141 numbered statements, definitions, problems, propositions, and rules. With its publication Kepler founded and named a new science, *dioptrics*, the science of refraction by lenses. Kepler had joined optics and astronomy in a permanent alliance.

Some of the drawings Kepler made to illustrate *Diop-*

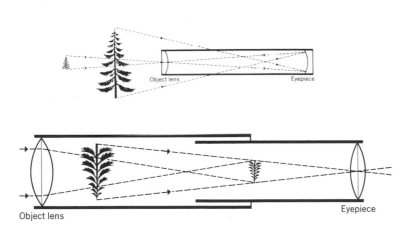

Kepler's Telescope

trice, including his sketch of the telescope, are still found in modern textbooks on geometrical optics.

If Kepler ever built his telescope, no trace of it remains, but others did build instruments like the one he proposed. One of these telescope makers was a Jesuit astronomer, Father Christoph Scheiner, who described his Keplerian telescope in a paper on sunspots published in 1630, the year Kepler died. After that time the "Scheiner telescope," built according to Kepler's diagram, became the model for astronomical telescopes everywhere.

Kepler spent his whole life struggling against poverty and illness. A man who delighted in the order and precision of mathematics, he spent his childhood in a disorderly household where he felt in the way most of the time. His father, Heinrich Kepler, deserted the family several times and finally disappeared permanently. His mother, Katharina, had such a talent for getting into trouble that she narrowly escaped being burned as a witch.

The son of this ill-matched couple, Johannes Kepler, was born two days after Christmas in 1571. In Weil, the small south German town where they lived, the Keplers were looked upon as a once-respectable family that had gone steadily downhill. Heinrich's father, Sebaldus, had been mayor of Weil, but by the time his grandson Johannes was born he had lost his position and his fortune.

Later, when he wrote about his childhood, Johannes Kepler remembered years of misery. At four, he wrote, "I almost died of smallpox, was in very ill health, and my hands were badly crippled." He remembered his father as "vicious, inflexible, quarrelsome and doomed to a bad end." His mother he described as "gossiping and quarrelsome" with a "bad disposition." He showed little affection for either parent when he wrote those words, but years later, when his mother was tried for witchcraft, he rushed to her defense and saved her from the stake.

Among his bitter memories there were a few bright spots. He remembered a comet he saw when he was six years old. "I heard much about the comet of that year, 1577, and was taken by my mother to a high place to look at it." And at nine, "I was called outside by my parents to look at the eclipse of the moon. It appeared quite red." He expressed no gratitude, but he must have had some feeling for his unfortunate parents, who had, after all, cared enough about him to show him a comet and an eclipse. They had introduced him to the wonders of the night sky, kindling a childhood interest that grew into a lifelong dedication to astronomy.

When Johannes was old enough to start his education he was sent to a school for craftsmen, to be taught a skill such as carpentry, metalworking, or weaving. The teachers soon recognized his quick bright mind and recommended that he be sent to a Latin school where he could be prepared for higher education. Such an exceptionally bright boy, so eager to learn, surely could become a teacher or a clergyman.

The Keplers had no money to pay for their son's education. Johannes might have had to stay in the trade school if they had not lived in the Duchy of Württemberg, where the Protestant dukes had set up an excellent system of free schools.

This was the time of the Reformation in Europe, when religious controversy was raging between the Catholics of the Holy Roman Church and the Protestant Lutherans. When the dukes of Württemberg had become Lutherans they had pledged themselves to spread the faith by educating superior Lutheran clergymen. For the future good of the church, they set up scholarships and grants "for the children of the poor and faithful who are of a diligent, Christian, and God-fearing disposition."

If Kepler's parents did not fit the description, their boy certainly did. He seemed naturally religious—a sensitive, serious boy who listened solemnly to the reading of the scriptures and asked thoughtful questions. His teachers looked into his future and imagined him a learned Lutheran minister. With the help of the dukes' scholarships Johannes Kepler's education was assured.

In the Latin school Kepler discovered mathematics and proved himself amazingly quick to grasp and solve difficult problems. At thirteen he entered a seminary at Adelberg and at seventeen was ready for the University of Tübingen, a leading center of Protestant scholarship.

At Tübingen Kepler had excellent teachers who recognized and appreciated his rare abilities, but he was unhappy. Like any other seventeen-year-old, he wanted some friends his own age. He had none. Even in the lower schools he had been unpopular with his fellow students, but he never accepted his unpopularity. At Tübingen he brooded about it.

"I suffered dreadfully and nearly died of my troubles," he wrote later. "The cause was my dishonor and the hatred of my school fellows whom I was driven by fear to denounce." He probably exaggerated the "hatred," but most of his schoolmates simply didn't understand his solemn approach to life. It made them uncomfortable.

Then quite unexpectedly he discovered a key to the kind of popularity he longed for. His schoolmates began to call him "Wizard," seeking him out to cast horoscopes for them and foretell their futures. His interest in the stars, combined with his gift for mathematics, and perhaps the influence of his mother's "witchcraft," made him a skillful astrologer.

Nowadays an astrologer is very different from an astronomer. Astrologers are fortune-tellers who say that a person's life and character are influenced by the positions of the moon, stars, and planets at the time he was born. Astronomers are scientists who study the sky, record their observations, and interpret them. In Kepler's time, when Europe was just emerging from the superstitious Middle Ages, most professional star-watchers had to be both astrologers and astronomers.

During Kepler's lifetime he was honored more for his astrology than for his contributions to science. He made his living primarily as an astrologer. This profession was respected, at that time, even by the Catholic church. The University of Rome had a professorship of astrology founded by Pope Leo X, and the teachings of St. Thomas Aquinas convinced Christians everywhere that the stars influenced their lives.

Medieval rulers had hired mathematicians to watch the skies—not because they were especially eager to learn about the stars, but because they expected foolproof advice. A century or two later, in Kepler's time, wealthy monarchs such as Rudolph II still believed firmly in the wisdom of their astrologers. Rudolph named Kepler Imperial Mathematican not as a reward for Kepler's phenomenal achievements in mathematical astronomy but for his predictions about wars, famines, epidemics, and even the emperor's health.

As he grew older Kepler was to become more and more critical of the pseudoscience that robbed him of time for genuine scientific pursuits. Astrology, he said, was "the stepdaughter of astronomy."

At Tübingen, however, astronomy's stepdaughter occupied some of young Kepler's time but never interfered with his studies. He was seriously determined to become a Lutheran minister and increasingly fascinated by mathematics and astronomy. His favorite teacher was Michael Maestlin, a leading astronomer and mathematician who recognized in the seventeen-year-old Kepler a first-rate scientific mind. Maestlin's respect for his pupil led him to share with Kepler an idea he had not dared to teach in the classroom.

A good Lutheran, Maestlin taught the official view that the sun traveled around a stationary earth. Privately he believed the Copernican theory that the sun was the center around which the earth revolved, a planet among other planets. A mind such as Kepler's, he felt, deserved a chance to examine this theory and evaluate it for himself.

When Kepler read Maestlin's copy of *On the Revolutions of the Heavenly Spheres* by Copernicus, he knew he had found the truth. He didn't know why; he simply *knew* what Copernicus said was true. For the next thirty years Kepler was to examine this truth—explaining, defending, and adding to it through mathematical proofs—until he gave the world three beautifully precise laws. These laws would describe exactly the planets' orbits around the sun, furnishing indisputable proof that Copernicus was right.

Kepler never forgot his gratitude to Michael Maestlin. He referred to him often in his writings as the man who guided him in his quest for truth. In later years Kepler kept up a correspondence with his old teacher, even after Maestlin stopped writing, because "I have nothing of the same value to offer in writing to such an outstanding mathematician."

In 1591, when he was twenty, Kepler completed his studies with the Tübingen Faculty of Arts. Still planning to become a minister, he spent three years more with the Faculty of Theology. He would have reached his goal in 1594, but fate and the faculty intervened before the final examinations.

A Protestant school in Graz, capital of the Catholic province of Styria, needed a teacher of mathematics and astronomy. Tübingen officials recommended Johannes Kepler. He accepted the assignment with the understanding that he would return to Tübingen later for his theological degree. He never did. Religion remained an important part of Kepler's life, but at Graz he found his real vocation. There were cosmic questions to be answered and he intended to answer them.

He had to know why the planets moved as they did around the sun. Why did some move faster than others? Did the size of their orbits affect their speeds? And why were there only six planets (no more were known at that time) instead of twenty or a hundred? He wanted to find orderly mathematical explanations for the motions of the planets and their relationships to each other.

Kepler's first steps in his search led him to publish a mystical theory which was entirely wrong but was impor-

The Copernican system, accepted by Kepler and Galileo, was rejected by the churches—both Catholic and Lutheran.

COPERNICANVM
Systema
TIVS CREATI
THESI
CANA IN
EXHIBITVM.

tant for several reasons. *The Cosmic Mystery*, published at Tübingen in 1596, described a solar system in which the orbits of the six known planets were determined by the shapes of the five perfect solids in Euclid's geometery, the only possible solid shapes having all faces exactly alike.

A diagram of Kepler's system looks like a child's toy, with pieces neatly nested one inside the other. The orbit of Saturn, he said, could be drawn on an invisible sphere which was the outer limit of the solar system. Into this sphere could be fitted an invisible cube which determined the orbit of Jupiter. A tetrahedron inside the cube determined the orbit of Mars; a dodecahedron, the Earth's orbit; an icosahedron, Venus's orbit; an octahedron, Mercury's orbit.

The system was elaborate nonsense but it contained the seeds of Kepler's future work. Also it was the first *published* defense of Copernicus by a professional astronomer. It attracted the attention of two important men who were to influence Kepler's life—Galileo in Italy and Tycho Brahe in Denmark.

Galileo was a thirty-three-year-old teacher at Padua when he received a copy of *The Cosmic Mystery* with a letter from the twenty-six-year-old Kepler. Galileo had never heard of Kepler, but the older man, whose defense of Copernicus in Italy was discouraged by the Church, was pleased to discover a fellow Copernican in Germany. He wrote a letter to the young teacher in Graz.

Dated August 4, 1597, the letter confessed: "I adopted the teachings of Copernicus many years ago . . . . however, so far I have not dared bring [this] into public light, frightened by the fate of Copernicus himself." He added,

"I would certainly dare to publish my reflections at once if more people like you existed; as they don't, I shall refrain from doing so." This was the beginning of a brief correspondence between the two mathematicians.

Kepler replied immediately, urging Galileo to speak up about his beliefs. He suggested that Galileo might have his works published in Germany if he had trouble getting them accepted in Italy. He received no answer from Galileo. When another letter remained unanswered Kepler assumed that their correspondence was over.

His relationship with the Danish astronomer Tycho Brahe was another matter. Since his student days at Tübingen Kepler had heard of Tycho and his palatial observatory, Uraniborg, on an island called Hveen, near Copenhagen. The first national observatory in the Western world, Uraniborg contained astronomical instruments as least ten times as accurate as any others in the world—and some were forty or fifty times as big. Kepler dreamed of visiting Uraniborg to work with these remarkable tools but he knew it was impossible. A thousand miles away! As remote as the moon for an underpaid teacher.

Kepler had little hope of meeting Tycho but he did write to him, and the great man answered. When *The Cosmic Mystery* was published Kepler sent a copy to Tycho. Whatever the Dane may have thought of Kepler's strange heavenly geometry, he was impressed with the young man's mathematical skill. Three years later, when he needed an assistant, he offered Kepler the job.

When the offer from Tycho arrived, Kepler could hardly believe his good luck. Tycho was no longer a thousand miles away but in Prague, just a few days away from Graz

Even as a student, Kepler had heard of Tycho Brahe and his wonderful observatory on the Danish island of Hveen.

by horseback or carriage. The Danish nobleman had left his country after a quarrel with King Christian IV and was presently Imperial Mathematician at the court of the Emperor Rudolph II. Now Kepler was invited to meet the great astronomer and work with him. He regretted that he would never see the fabulous Uraniborg, but one look at Tycho's star charts could speed up his own work with the orbits of the planets. Kepler accepted Tycho's offer.

His opportunity could not have come at a better time. All Lutherans had been driven out of Graz by the Catholic Archduke Ferdinand. Kepler was later called back to cast a "calendar" (horoscope) for the province, but he had heard enough about Lutherans tortured as heretics to make him decide to leave as soon as he could.

At Benatek Castle in Prague, Kepler and Tycho met for the first time in February 1600. They worked together for twenty-one months until Tycho's death at the age of fifty-five, in October 1601. A few days later Kepler was named Tycho's successor as Imperial Mathematician.

Kepler continued to work on the first assignment Tycho had given him, to calculate the orbit of Mars. Kepler had boasted at first that with the help of Tycho's charts he could do the job in eight days. It took six years. His patient, disciplined calculations, repeated over and over as often as a hundred times, led him eventually to find that Mars' orbit was elliptical. His discovery was totally unexpected. Even Copernicus had assumed that planets traveled in perfect circles. Kepler proved that Mars, at least, did not describe a circle at all but an elongated orbit, an ellipse. He had destroyed his own theories set forth in *The Cosmic Mystery*, but Kepler was concerned with finding truth.

In solving the riddle, he discovered two laws of planetary motion still used by astronomers in the Space Age:

KEPLER'S FIRST LAW: *The path of a planet around the sun is an ellipse, with the sun at one focal point.*
KEPLER'S SECOND LAW: *A line drawn from the sun to a planet will sweep over equal areas in equal times.*

A detailed account of Kepler's trial-and-error approach to the truth about Mars was published in 1609 in a heavy volume with the Latin title, *Astronomia Nova* (New Astronomy). A copy of the book was sent to Galileo, who didn't

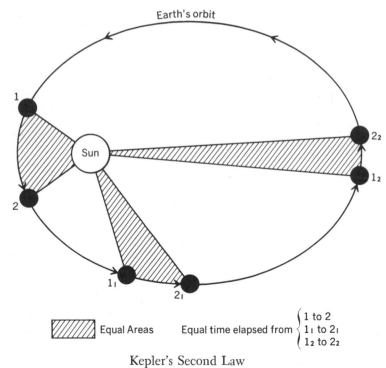

Kepler's Second Law

acknowledge it. It was a few months later in the spring of
1610 that Kepler received from Galileo the copy of his
Message from the Stars, the book that inspired Kepler's
later experiments with lenses described in *Dioptrice*.

Two years later Rudolph II died, owing Kepler thousands
of florins in unpaid salary. The former Imperial Mathematician left Prague for Austria to accept a modest post as
teacher and district mathematician in Linz. His first wife,
Barbara, had died in Prague after a long illness. Now the
forty-one-year-old Kepler married again. His bride was a
much younger woman, twenty-four-year-old Susanna Reuttinger, whom he chose after listing eleven "candidates" and
casting horoscopes for five of them. This marriage turned
out to be much happier than his first, which had been more
or less arranged for him by colleagues at Graz.

During his fourteen years in Linz Kepler completed two
more major works and started several others. His *Harmony
of the World*, published in 1619, introduced his third law.

KEPLER'S THIRD LAW: *If you compare the average distance
of each planet from the sun with the length of time it
takes to go once around the sun, the cube of the distance is
proportional to the square of the time.*

Astronomers simplify this statement by letting D represent the planet's average distance from the sun and T represent the time of one revolution. Then they can say that the
ratio of D cubed to T squared, or $\frac{D^3}{T^2}$ is the same for
every planet. In other words, there is a *definite mathematical relationship* between the distance of a planet from the
sun and the time it takes to go once around the sun. Every

planet obeys the same law. Today this is a fact that any student takes for granted, but in Kepler's day it was a revelation. Isaac Newton, half a century later, used it as a stepping stone to his Law of Universal Gravitation.

Kepler's work at Linz also included a controversial three-volume textbook, the *Epitome of Copernican Astronomy*. Long after his death Kepler's book brought about the revolution in the teaching of astronomy that Copernicus had foreseen in 1543.

In another book Kepler anticipated today's science fiction. Off and on, from 1609 until his death in 1630, Kepler worked on a tale he called *Somnium* (A Dream). It was about a boy named Duracotus who traveled to the moon. Kepler never finished it, but the fragment—with pages of valuable scientific notes—was published in Latin in 1634. A new English translation appeared in 1965.

Kepler's final work at Linz, while the Thirty Years' War raged around him, was an attempt to complete Tycho's star charts. With characteristic generosity toward the emperor who never paid his debts, Kepler called these charts the *Rudolphine Tables*. They were being printed in 1626 when Linz was seized by Lutheran peasants during a bloody revolt, and the printing presses were smashed. Kepler gathered up his precious tables and took them to Ulm, where the printing was completed the following year in time for the Frankfurt Fair. The *Rudolphine Tables* were welcomed by navigators as the first dependable star guide for ships. The modern *Nautical Almanac* is a descendant of these tables.

While he was in Ulm, Kepler had left his family with friends in Regensburg (formerly Ratisbon). After the publication of the tables, he neither sent for them nor returned to them immediately. Feeling depressed about everything—the war, his work, his health and his finances—he wandered about aimlessly until the duke of Wallenstein offered him a position as his personal *mathematicus*. This meant casting more horoscopes, but Kepler was desperate for a job. He accepted the duke's offer and moved his family to the Duchy of Sagan.

As soon as he began his new duties Kepler realized that he had made a mistake. He hated the job, but his health was failing and he had to provide for his family. Two months before his sixtieth birthday, Kepler told his wife he couldn't stand the thought of dying in Sagan. Suddenly one morning he saddled his horse and set out to find work somewhere else. A letter to a friend dated October 31, 1630, shows that he went to Leipzig. Two days later he was in Regensburg, where a friend took him in and persuaded him to rest. The friend, a Lutheran preacher named Jacob Fischer, described his last days:

Our Kepler arrived in this town on an old jade (which he subsequently sold for two florins). He was only three days here when he was taken ill with a feverish ailment. . . . Soon his mind became clouded with ever-rising fever. He did not talk like one in possession of his faculties. . . . In his last agony, as he gave up his ghost to God, a Protestant clergyman of Regensburg, Sigismund Christopher Donavarus, a relative of mine, consoled him in a manly way, as behooves a servant of God. This happened on November 15, 1630. On the nineteenth he was buried in the cemetery of St. Peter, outside the town.

A few years later, as the Thirty Years' War continued, Regensburg was bombarded and the cemetery was destroyed. Kepler's tombstone disappeared, but his work remains a lasting monument. Space Age astronomers, physicists, engineers, and mathematicians are still building on the foundations laid by Johannes Kepler.

About thirty-four years after Kepler's death one of his works made a vital contribution to the future of science when a copy of A *Supplement to Vitellio* was read by a third-year student at Cambridge in England. The twenty-one-year-old student was Isaac Newton.

3

ISAAC NEWTON'S
REFLECTING TELESCOPE

Isaac Newton read Kepler's book on optics because he wanted to build a better telescope. After three years of exploring geometry, astronomy, alchemy, and theology at Trinity College, Cambridge, he was now delving into optics. It was the spring of 1664 and he was twenty-one, full of ideas and questions about everything he was learning.

He had bought a small telescope and was spending nearly every clear night outdoors, studying the moon in all its phases. When the moon was full, it was bright enough to obscure the stars, too bright for the kind of prolonged watching that Isaac indulged in. His eyes burned and his head ached. The strain on his eyes was made even worse by the rainbow-colored blurs that appeared around the moon when he viewed it through his telescope. The colored fringes were always there—around planets, stars, or any other bright object within range of the telescope.

Isaac spent hours adjusting the tube of his instrument, trying to bring into focus a sharp clear image without the rainbow fringe. The more he tried, the more he strained his eyes and suffered painful headaches.

Isaac Newton (1642–1727).

Newton spoke to his tutor Isaac Barrow about the colored phenomenon and asked how it could be corrected. Barrow told him that the colored fringes were probably inevitable, the price one paid for the magnifying power of the telescope. Other sky watchers had suffered headaches too and had tried to improve the design of telescopes. Experimenters had tried wider lenses for probing deeper into the heavens, but wider lenses simply made the rainbow distortions worse. This was why there were no really big telescopes. The world's best instruments at that time were long skinny tubes requiring elaborate supports, or even "air" telescopes consisting of suspended lenses without tubes.

Professor Barrow suggested that his pupil read a book by Johannes Kepler, *A Supplement to Vitellio*, popularly called Kepler's *Optics*. Kepler, too, had been curious about colored light. Perhaps his book could answer Isaac Newton's questions.

Newton took his tutor's advice and read Kepler's book, determined to remove the built-in rainbow from telescopes. He succeeded eventually, but not until after he had made fundamental discoveries in optics, physics, and mathematics. These discoveries changed the direction of science and gave Newton's name to an age.

When Newton first turned the pages of Kepler's *Optics*, he found no clear-cut directions for building a better telescope, but he did find answers to many of his questions. What excited him even more were the unanswered questions. Each one was a challenge, a riddle to be solved, and he would not put them out of his mind until he had solved them all.

Meanwhile, in January 1665 he received his Bachelor of

Arts degree from Trinity College, along with twenty-five others. His classmates later remembered him as a solitary, not very friendly young man who complained when his roommate's friends were loud and rowdy. They joked about his absent-mindedness and found him rather stiff and solemn. He was certainly not sociable, but apparently he allowed himself to unbend a little at graduation time. One of his student notebooks, still preserved, shows that his expenses included, at about that time, fifteen shillings "lost at cards" and three shillings and sixpence spent at the tavern. Ninepence went to his "chamberfellow" as payment for "a broken glass and other things."

If Newton took a little time out from his studies, the interruption was brief. During the six months after graduation he worked furiously—reading, experimenting, calculating. He ground lenses of various shapes and worked out his own system of mathematics for measuring the areas within their curves. A tentative description of this system of "fluxions," dated May 20, 1665, is still preserved in his school notebook. Years later the method became the integral and differential calculus, the first efficient method for calculating changing rates and quantities.

At the Stourbridge Fair Newton had bought a prism and had begun a series of experiments. Like Kepler, he wanted to measure the bending of a beam of light as it passed through the prism. These experiments led him eventually to the first scientific explanation of the colored light of the spectrum. In 1665 he suspected the truth—that white light is made up of many colors, each of which bends at a different angle when passed from one medium into another. He suspected it, but he couldn't prove it.

When the problem of the stubborn rainbow fringes seen through the telescope remained unsolved, Newton decided to try a different approach. He had learned that *reflected* light would bounce off a shiny surface in straight lines. It was not bent (refracted) and did not produce colored blurs. Perhaps he could build a telescope that would gather light without bending it through a lens. Perhaps a mirror could catch the light of the moon and bounce it toward the eye without producing colored distortions. Newton made a note of his idea and resolved to come back to it later.

In 1665 the seeds of Newton's greatest discoveries were taking root, but they needed time to grow. His mind was boiling over with new ideas, questions, riddles to be solved. He wanted time to sort out his thoughts, to digest what he had learned, to explore new corridors of learning. The opportunity came unexpectedly in August 1665.

That summer a sudden outbreak of bubonic plague was devastating London. Thousands of people were dying every day and the disease was spreading outside the city. Cambridge was close enough to London to be in danger. The university officials had read historical accounts of the sinister Black Death of the fourteenth century—bubonic plagues that destroyed one-fourth of the population of Europe. Without waiting for the London plague to reach Cambridge, officials closed the university and sent the students home.

For Isaac Newton home was in Woolsthorpe, a little village in Lincolnshire, seven miles south of Grantham. There wasn't much in Woolsthorpe—not even a church. There were three or four small farms, a few thatched cottages, and the modest old gray stone manor house where

Isaac Newton's birthplace at Woolsthorpe, Lincolnshire.

Newton was born on Christmas 1642. The house had belonged to his grandfather, Robert Newton, who had bought it from a man named Underwood when it was already at least one hundred and fifty years old.

Isaac's father, also named Isaac, had inherited the manor house from his father in 1641. The following year he had married Hannah Ayscough and had brought his bride to Woolsthorpe. He never saw his remarkable son. He died at the age of thirty-seven, two months before Isaac was born.

Isaac Newton's father was remembered as a "wild, extravagant, and weak man," but his mother was admired and respected in the community. A relative later described her as "a woman of so extraordinary an understanding, virtue, and goodness, that those who think that a soul like Sir Isaac

62

Newton's could be formed by anything less than the immediate operation of a Divine Creator might be apt to ascribe
it to her."

As an infant Isaac was underweight and physically weak.
When he was about two years old his mother remarried.
Her new husband, the Reverend Barnabas Smith, was rector
of a church in North Witham, a village about a mile south
of Woolsthorpe. When Hannah Ayscough Newton Smith
moved to her new home in North Witham, she left her son
at Woolsthorpe with his maternal grandmother, under the
guardianship of his uncle, James Ayscough.

Until he was twelve Isaac attended schools in Skillington
and Stoke, villages within walking distance of the manor
house. Then he was sent to the King's School in Grantham,
a town important enough to be the headquarters for a
bishop.

During the school term he lived with a family named
Clark, friends of his mother. Isaac had every reason to enjoy
the arrangement. Mr. Clark was an apothecary who mixed
mysterious compounds from the powdered and liquid chem-
icals stored in a marvelous collection of bottles and jars on
the shelves of his shop. Isaac was fascinated by Mr. Clark's
work, and the apothecary encouraged his interest by allow-
ing him to watch the mixing process and teaching him the
names of various ingredients. This early interest in chemis-
try stayed with Newton all his life.

The Clarks provided a study for Isaac and gave him
plenty of books. Mrs. Clark's daughter by a former marriage, a girl about Isaac's age, became his best friend during
the years at Grantham. Her first name seems to have been
lost to history, but "Miss Storey" was remembered by New-

ton as an important influence in his life. She was intelligent, gentle, and interested in subjects that interested him. She admired the mechanical toys he built and encouraged him to build more.

Years later, one of Newton's Grantham schoolmates recalled some of the working models he had built. His description is still preserved among the Newton Papers at Cambridge. He told about a small windmill:

This sometimes he would set upon the housetop where he lodged, and clothing [covering] it with sailcloth, the wind would readily turn it; but what was most extraordinary in its composition was, that he put a mouse into it, which he called the miller, and that the mouse made the mill turn round when he pleased; and he would joke too upon the miller eating the corn that was put in.

The same schoolmate also remembered a water clock

he made out of a box he begged of Mr. Clark's wife's brother. As described to me, it resembled pretty much our common clocks and clock-cases, but less; for it was not above four feet in height and of proportional breadth. There was a dial plate at the top with figures of the hours. The index was turned by a piece of wood, which either rose or fell by water dropping. This stood in the room where he lay and he took care every morning to supply it with its proper quantity of water; and the family upon occasion would go to see what was the hour by it. It was left in the house long after he went away to the University.

The years at Grantham were exciting ones for Isaac Newton, but suddenly, at sixteen, the direction of his life changed. His stepfather died and his mother returned to Woolsthorpe with her three younger children, Benjamin,

Mary, and Hannah Smith. The Reverend Mr. Smith had left her a comfortable income, but a farm was attached to the rectory and she could not manage it alone. She sent for her son to help her.

Isaac returned to Woolsthorpe, but he had no talent for farming and even less enthusiasm. It was pleasant to take a book into the field when he was sent to watch the cattle or the sheep, but he usually became so absorbed in what he was reading that the animals wandered away before he noticed them and he had to call for help to round them up again.

When he and a servant were sent to Grantham on Saturdays to sell the farm's produce, he would tell the servant to take care of things. He would go back to the Clarks' house to spend the day in the attic with a pile of old books. Since he never noticed the time, the servant would have to come looking for him when it was necessary to go home. Finally Isaac's mother decided that her son was not meant to be a farmer.

In the fall of 1660 she sent him back to Grantham to be tutored for college. For the next few months, until he was admitted to Trinity College on June 5, 1661, Isaac was back in his old room at the Clarks', free to read as late as he liked, with no interruptions for milking cows or herding sheep. More than ever he appreciated Miss Storey's sympathetic companionship. When he left for Cambridge, they were engaged to be married.

Between terms at Cambridge, whenever he came home for a holiday, Isaac went to Grantham to see his fiancée. But when he was exiled to Woolsthorpe because of the plague, he made up his mind to break the engagement.

Now he knew what he wanted to do with his life. He had to give *all* his attention to the cosmic riddles he wanted to solve—and he would have to work alone. He explained his feelings to Miss Storey, who eventually accepted the idea. In her old age she told Newton's friend Dr. Stukeley that "it was incompatible with his fortunes to marry; perhaps his studies, too." She and Isaac remained good friends and he continued to visit her whenever he was at home, even after she married a Mr. Vincent. She was the first and only woman Newton showed any interest in, until he was past sixty years old and proposed to a widow who refused him. He never married.

While the plague scourged London, Isaac Newton made the most of the interruption in his Cambridge career. Woolsthorpe was isolated and quiet, and he could spend most of his time alone. He was free of any marriage plans, free of classroom lectures and lessons, free of the farm chores which his mother had finally assigned to others. He had time to think, and there was so much he wanted to think about—all his questions about light, lenses, alchemy, mathematics, gravity, and the moon.

This enforced vacation was the most productive period of Newton's life. One extravagant historian calls it "the most fruitful eighteen months in all the history of the creative imagination."

During this period—and the months at Cambridge just before the plague—he discovered fundamental truths about the nature of white light, laid the foundation for the calculus, and formulated his "inverse square" law, which became the Law of Universal Gravitation.

Looking back at those remarkable years, Newton later recalled how much he had accomplished: "All this was during the two plague years of 1665 and 1666, for in those days I was in the prime of my age for invention, and minded mathematics and philosophy more than at any time since."

Soon after he arrived at Woolsthorpe, Newton resumed his experiments with lenses and prisms. The series of prism experiments he had begun at Cambridge had led him to the tantalizing hypothesis he wanted to prove: that any beam of white light is made up of all the colors of the spectrum. Johannes Kepler had toyed with this idea but had never been able to prove it. Newton succeeded in finding a proof, discovering at the same time that each color is bent by a prism at a different and definite angle. Once he had made this discovery, he put his notes aside and went on to the next problem. He told nobody about his findings.

"During the same year," Newton wrote later, "I began to think of gravity extending to the orb of the moon." The familiar story about Isaac Newton and the apple is supposed to have happened at this time. According to legend, it was a falling apple that inspired the Law of Gravitation. If we can believe Newton's early biographers, including the French philosopher Voltaire, the story was more than a legend. Voltaire said he heard it from Newton's favorite niece, Catharine Barton, who kept house for her uncle during the last years of his life.

Some versions of the story make it seem that Newton saw the apple fall and immediately, in a flash, perceived the Universal Law, complete with mathematical equations. It was, of course, not that simple. The complicated mathematical process was carried out gradually, through patient trial and error, using Newton's own system of "fluxions."

It is possible a falling apple gave him a valuable clue.

Newton may have asked himself why the moon didn't fall as the apple did. What kept it up there, as if it were tied to the earth by an invisible string? The moon was like a ball tied to a string, being whirled in circles. If the string should break, the ball would fly off in a straight line. Why didn't the moon fly off into space? It must be tied to the earth by some powerful force. Could it be the same force that pulled down the apple? If so, then he came back to the same nagging question—why didn't the moon fall? Could it possibly be because it was so far away from the earth? If it were closer, would it fall?

Each question led Newton to another, and he investigated them all. By the time he was through he had worked out a rule for measuring the earth's attraction for the moon and had applied this rule to everything else in the universe. He had proved to his own satisfaction that every particle in the universe—not just on earth—is attracted to every other particle with a measurable force. The amount of force depends not upon the *weight* of the bodies, but upon their relative *mass*—the amount of material that makes them up.

Weight is, after all, simply another way of measuring the force of gravity. It changes according to the distance of an object from the center of the earth. If the object is far enough away, it has no weight at all—as Space Age astronauts have discovered—but it still has mass.

Newton did not pretend to know what gravity was, but he could tell precisely how it behaved:

Every body of matter in the universe attracts every other body with a force that is directly proportional to the prod-

uct of the masses of the two bodies and inversely propor-
tional to the square of the distance between them.

To find this law Newton had referred to the work of
Galileo and Kepler. The result was an astonishing synthesis
of the greatest discoveries of both men. If Newton realized
what he had done, he said nothing about it. The Law of
Gravitation remained his secret for nearly twenty years
longer.

By the time he returned to Cambridge in the spring of
1667, when he was still only twenty-four, Newton had made
the discoveries that would change the direction of science.
He mentioned none of his accomplishments except "fluxions."

Newton told his tutor Isaac Barrow that he had worked
out some problems by a new system that might interest the
older man. When he showed Barrow the paper about fluxions he had written in May 1665, the tutor urged Newton
to develop the system and publish it. Newton, always unaccountably secretive about his work, did nothing of the
kind. But Barrow was impressed and watched Newton carefully as he became first a fellow of Trinity College, then
Master of Arts.

Two years later, in 1669, Barrow told university authorities that Newton was far superior to him as a mathematician and recommended that the younger man succeed him
as Lucasian Professor of Mathematics at Cambridge. Barrow returned to the theological studies he preferred and
Newton, at twenty-seven, held the most respected chair of
mathematics in England.

The professorship was not demanding. He was required to deliver only one lecture a week, so he had plenty of time to continue his own research in any of the fields that interested him. He was not a popular lecturer. Sometimes only a handful of students gathered to hear him. He was so absentminded or so absorbed in his other work, that he often forgot to show up in the lecture hall. But while he and his students were staying away from the classroom, Newton completed his telescope—the instrument that became a model for the world's greatest telescopes for the next three centuries.

By modern standards it was a tiny instrument—just six inches long and about an inch across—fashioned with the same skill and care he had devoted to the mechanical toys he built as a boy. The unusual feature of this telescope was that it had no lens at the front of the tube. Instead, the front of the tube was open and a concave mirror was placed at the back of the tube to gather light.

The image of a star or planet was reflected by this metal mirror to a second mirror, a small flat reflecting plate inside the tube, near the front, inclined at a 45-degree angle so as to throw the image up through a hole in the side of the tube. This hole was fitted with an eyepiece containing the only lens in the whole telescope—a tiny plano-convex lens to magnify the image; which appeared with *no* colored fringe.

When Isaac Barrow saw Newton's model he urged the shy inventor to put aside his reticence for once and let people know what he had done. Newton protested that it wasn't really *his* idea. He had read about a reflecting tele-

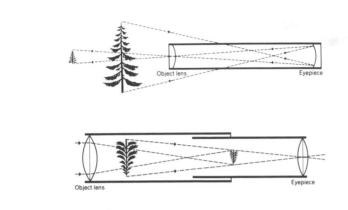

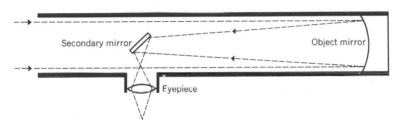

Newton's Reflecting Telescope

scope designed in 1663 by James Gregory, a Scottish mathematician. Gregory's telescope had an eyepiece at the back, fitted into a hole in the center of the light-gathering mirror. Newton had tried this design but discovered that it wasted too much light. So he devised his own improvement on Gregory's idea, eliminating the hole in the mirror. It was

71

true that Gregory had never built a practical model of his invention, so Newton's instrument was actually the first workable reflecting telescope.

Barrow respected Newton's modesty, but he thought it would do no harm to let other scientists know about the telescope. Somehow the Royal Society of London for improving Natural Knowledge, Britain's version of the Lincean

Newton's little reflector, which he built in 1671, is displayed in the library of the Royal Society in London.

Academy of Galileo's time, heard about Newton's instrument and asked him to send the model to London.

Newton, the perfectionist, was not satisfied with his first model. He apologized for his 6-inch telescope because "by reason of.bad materials and for want of good polish, it represents not things so distinct as a six feet tube will do; yet I think it will discover as much as any three or four feet tube, especially if the objects be luminous." So he built another model, which he considered better, and sent it to the Royal Society late in 1671.

The members of the Royal Society responded by electing him to membership on January 11, 1672. Newton, now the newest fellow, was invited to contribute a scientific paper.

Three weeks later his paper "On the Composition of White Light" was read to the Royal Society. It was a simple, straightforward description of his prism experiments, telling what he had discovered about the "unequal refrangibility" of the different colors of light that make up a beam of white light. This time the response to Newton's work was anything but unanimously favorable.

Some scientists hailed Newton as a genius. Others were disappointed because he had not told them what light *is*, but had merely described its behavior. News of the controversy spread to other centers of learning. All over Europe scientists were taking sides. The shy professor had become famous—and he hated it.

Fame invaded his privacy, took too much time away from his work, and forced him to write letters to people who disagreed with him. Longing for anonymity, Newton wrote to the Royal Society, "I hope you will not take it ill if you find me never doing anything more in that kind."

I have perused yoᵉ very ingenious Theory of Vision in wch (to be free wth you as a friend should be) there seems to be some things more solid & satisfactory, other more disputable but yet plausibly suggested & well deserving yᵗ consideration of yᵗ ingenious. The more satisfactory I take to be your asserting yᵗ we see wth both eyes at once, yoᵉ speculation about yᵗ use of yᵉ *musculus obliquus inferior*, yoᵉ assigning every fibre in yᵉ optick nerve of one eye to have its correspondent in yᵗ of yᵗ other, both wch make all things appear to both eyes in one & yᵗ same place & yoᵉ solving hereby yᵗ duplicity of yᵗ object in distorted eyes & confuting yᵗ childish opinion about yᵗ splitting yᵗ optick cone.

Js. N

Trin. Coll Cambridge
20ᵗʰ 1682

Fragment of a letter written by Newton in 1682.

After that, Newton became more secretive than ever about his work. Retreating to his Cambridge study, he avoided attention and published nothing else for fifteen years after the paper on white light. But he was not idle, and his devotion to the scientific method demanded that he keep notes of his experiments and discoveries. Eventually the world had to find out what he was doing.

Meanwhile astronomers were still searching for an efficient mathematical rule to account for the movements of the planets. They had no way of knowing that Newton had already solved the problem, during the plague years at Woolsthorpe, and had even devised a *universal* law to explain the whole orchestration of the heavens. At the time, Newton had felt that his figures would "answer pretty nearly," but were not precise enough to constitute a proof. When his findings were finally brought to light, nearly twenty years after they were made, it was because of a friendly bet among three members of the Royal Society of London.

In the early spring of 1684 Christopher Wren (now more famous as the builder of St. Paul's Cathedral in London than as a scientist) was discussing planetary motion with two fellow scientists, Robert Hooke and Edmund Halley. The three agreed that the French mathematician Descartes' theory, that the planets were moved by whirlpools of "ether," was far less convincing than an "inverse-square" theory, according to which a planet is attracted to the sun by a force inversely proportional to the square of its distance from the sun.

The idea was not entirely new. In the sixty-five years since Kepler had first suggested a definite mathematical relationship between the distance of a planet from the sun and the time it takes to go once around the sun, many leading astronomers and mathematicians had studied his theory. Some had used it to derive other theories—such as this inverse-square measure of the sun's attraction—but they still considered Kepler's statement *no more* than a theory. Nobody had been able to prove it by calculation until Isaac

Newton did it with his system of "fluxions." But in 1684, only Newton knew that he had done it.

During the conversation with Wren and Halley, Robert Hooke boasted that he could calculate a proof showing that if the sun pulls a planet with a force calculated according to the inverse-square theory, the planet would travel in an ellipse. Wren offered him forty shillings to produce the proof within a given time. After several months had passed and Hooke had said nothing more about his proof, Halley suggested that Isaac Newton might be able to do it. He was certainly the best mathematician in England, and Halley had heard of Newton's new mathematical system called "fluxions."

On an August day in 1684 Halley went to Cambridge. Without mentioning his discussions with Wren and Hooke, he presented his question to Newton. What would be the shape of a planet's orbit, Halley asked, if the planet were attracted to the sun by a force which increased in inverse proportion to the square of its distance from the sun?

Newton answered without hesitation, "An ellipse."

Halley was astonished. How did Newton know?

"I have calculated it," Newton told him.

When Halley asked to see the figures of his proof, Newton said absent-mindedly that he couldn't find them just then, but he would be glad to calculate the proof again. Shortly afterward Halley received from Newton two different proofs of the elliptic orbit, following an inverse-square law.

Newton's enthusiasm for problems of planetary motion was aroused all over again. He spent the rest of the summer composing a course of nine lectures to be delivered under the title "De Motu Corporum" (On the Motion of Bodies). In November he sent a copy of his demonstrations to Halley.

As soon as he read Newton's manuscript Halley recognized the treasure it contained. It would be unthinkable for Newton to hide such knowledge any longer. He insisted that Newton publish his findings. Newton was reluctant to expose himself again to public attention, but Halley prodded him. The shy genius spent the next year and a half setting down his discoveries. The result was a heavy 250,000-word manuscript in Latin, *Philosophiae Naturalis Principia Mathematica* (Mathematical Principles of Natural Philosophy), later called simply the *Principia*.

The work was packed with revelations. It established a new science of *dynamics*, the study of how things move, still taught in first-year physics classes. It explained how the moon affects the tides and how the planets move around the sun. It made the surprising suggestion that comets travel in closed orbits—long, cigar-shaped ellipses. Astronomers had assumed that comets shot off into space and never returned. Halley later used Newton's rule to predict accurately the regular return of "his" comet of 1681—in 1758, 1835, and 1910. It is due again in 1986.

The Royal Society praised Newton's manuscript when they saw the first part of it, but said there were no funds for publishing it. Halley indignantly took the manuscript, collected enough money to publish it himself, and was able to send Newton first proofs in June 1686, while the final section was still being written. When the *Principia* was published in July 1687, Newton was hailed by the world's scientists as the new dictator of scientific thought. The work was so conclusive that no one was able to argue with him.

In spite of his fame Newton was in no hurry to publish

Edmund Halley used Newton's Law of Universal Gravitation to prove that the comet of 1682 was the same comet seen in 1607, 1531, 1456, and 1305. He predicted its return in 1758—and approximately every seventy-five years thereafter. This photograph was made on May 12, 1910. Halley's comet is due again in 1986.

anything else. Twenty years had passed between the time he laid the groundwork for his Universal Law and its publication in the *Principia*. Thirty years elapsed from the time he set down his system of fluxions in a school notebook until it was published, in part, by another English mathematician, John Wallis. An even longer period, thirty-eight years, separated Newton's prism experiments at Woolsthorpe in 1666 and the publication in 1704 of *Opticks*, his great work on light and lenses.

In his later years Newton was plunged into public life—whether he liked it or not. He served as a member of Parliament, was appointed Warden of the Mint, and was then promoted to Master of the Mint, with the task of reforming the coinage of England. The government job made it necessary for him to leave his Cambridge solitude and move to London.

He was fifty-four years old when he began this new life, but not too old to enjoy the change, once he accepted it. At first he was crotchety and retiring, but after a while he became quite sociable. His pretty niece Catharine Barton kept house for him. She loved to give dinner parties for her uncle and his friends, including distinguished men in government and the arts, as well as science.

In 1705, just after the publication of *Opticks*, he was knighted by Queen Anne and became *Sir* Isaac Newton. He also served as president of the Royal Society from 1703 until his death at eighty-five on March 20, 1727. He was buried in Westminster Abbey.

Even in his old age, Isaac Newton was concerned with telescope making. In the second edition of *Opticks*, published in 1717, he added a note about telescopes:

If the theory of making telescopes could at length be fully brought into practice, yet would there be certain bounds beyond which telescopes could not perform. For the air through which we look upon the stars is in a perpetual tremor. . . . The only remedy is a most serene and quiet air, such as may perhaps be found on the tops of the highest mountains, above the grosse clouds.

Today, in the "serene and quiet air" of Palomar Mountain, California, the world's largest Newtonian telescope probes the sky. Its giant mirror is two hundred inches across, but it is built on the same principle as Newton's tiny model with its one-inch mirror.

Newton's little telescope is still on display in the library of the Royal Society in London. An inscription reads: "Invented by Sir Isaac Newton and made with his own hands, 1671."

4

WILLIAM HERSCHEL'S
GIANT REFLECTORS

Astronomers admired Newton's reflecting telescope, but
most of them went on using refractors until an imaginative
amateur showed them what could be done with Newton's
instrument if it were built on a large scale. William Herschel explored the sky with telescopes that were forty, sixty,
and even eighty times the size of Newton's model. He built
them himself, set them up in his English garden, and
probed deep into the heavens to discover stars, comets, and
galaxies never seen before.

During the eighty-four years of his lifetime Herschel lived
two full lives—one as a German musician, the other as a
world-acclaimed English astronomer and telescope maker.
Music and astronomy shared his attention for many years,
until a spectacular discovery committed the rest of his life
to the stars.

In 1781, when he was forty-three years old, Herschel discovered a new planet, Uranus—the first such discovery since
ancient times. Five planets besides the earth had been
known since the beginnings of recorded history, but Friedrich Wilhelm Herschel—music teacher, organist, choir-

William Herschel (1738–1822).

master, and composer—discovered another member of the sun's family beyond distant Saturn. The discovery ended his musical career and introduced to the world of science William Herschel of Bath, an English astronomer who intended to map the position of every star he could find with his powerful telescopes.

Friedrich Wilhelm Herschel was born on November 15, 1738, in Hanover, a Prussian city now in Germany. He was the third child of Isaac and Anna Herschel, a hard-working German couple who lived modestly near the barracks of the Hanoverian Guards. Isaac was an oboist in the Guards band, a talented musician who taught himself to play several musical instruments and later taught his six children. The four boys—Jacob, Wilhelm, Alexander, and Dietrich—all became professional musicians. Sophia, the elder of their two sisters, followed her mother's advice and became a proper housewife and mother. Caroline, the younger girl, wanted a career as a concert singer, but her destiny was in astronomy, as assistant to her famous brother and later as an astronomer in her own right.

When Wilhelm was only four his father had a miniature violin made for him. The boy later remembered being lifted to a table top and asked to play a solo for guests. When he started school Wilhelm's quick intelligence was immediately noticed by his teachers. He was particularly good at arithmetic and was often asked by the schoolmaster to help the other pupils.

By the time he was fourteen Wilhelm had to leave school to earn money for the family. A musician in a military band made very little money, and Isaac Herschel had a hard time supporting his wife and six children. Jacob, the oldest boy, had joined his father in the band as soon as he was of age. When Wilhelm, too, was hired as an oboist for the band, Jacob was appointed organist at a church. Since both boys were earning enough money to lift some of the burden from their father, Isaac thought they deserved to spend some of it on their own education.

Isaac Herschel had many interests—philosophy, mathematics, astronomy, and literature, as well as music—and he wanted his children to appreciate learning for its own sake. He arranged for both boys to take French lessons from a tutor named Hofschlager, a highly educated man who shared many of Isaac's varied interests.

Hofschlager was so impressed with Wilhelm's alert mind that he found himself giving lessons in philosophy, logic, and history, as well as French. Later in his life Wilhelm remembered Hofschlager as an important influence on him.

To this fortunate circumstance it was undoubtedly owing [he wrote] that although I loved music to excess and made considerable progress in it, yet I determined with a sort of enthusiasm to devote every moment I could spare to the pursuit of knowledge, which I regard as the sovereign good, and in which I resolved to place all my future views of happiness in life.

The pursuit of knowledge did occupy the rest of his life. Circumstances led him straight into a successful career in music, but intellectual pursuits caused him to veer into another path—the path that led him to the stars.

It was as a musician that Wilhelm Herschel first visited England, the country which later claimed him as its own genius of astronomy. War had broken out in 1755 between France and England, and Prussia had sided with England.

During the Seven Years' War the Hanoverian Guards and their marching band were sent to England. Wilhelm Herschel and his oboe arrived in England with the rest of the band in April 1756.

The eighteen-year-old German visitor spoke no English, but he was so interested in finding out everything he could about the strange country that he soon learned enough to make himself understood among the Englishmen he met. He liked people and found it easy to make friends. The English were charmed by his enthusiasm and friendliness and invited him to their homes to meet their families. Pretty English girls offered to teach him the language and found him a quick learner.

While Herschel was enjoying English hospitality, he may have been able to forget why he was there. The war was something people talked about, but the young musician saw little military action. For him, the tour of duty in England was a pleasant vacation.

The following year his vacation ended when the Hanoverian Guards went home again. Wilhelm soon had a taste of battle, with all its violence and discomfort. Slogging around in mud and rain, sleeping in ditches, trying to play on a waterlogged instrument while gunfire drowned out the music—all of it seemed senseless to him. He was not a soldier anyway; he would never have chosen the military life; and he wasn't even sure what the fighting was about.

His father understood Wilhelm's feelings and sympathized. Isaac's own health had been ruined during the years of military service, but he felt he had to stay with the band. He had a wife and young children to support, and his job with the band was the only living he could be sure of. But

Wilhelm, he said, was free to go whenever he liked. He had no obligation to the Hanoverian Guards. When he had joined the band he had been so young that he was never properly sworn in, so he could not be called a deserter if he left. Besides, the musicians were just in the way during the fighting. Who would notice if one of them simply slipped away?

Before taking his father's advice Wilhelm went home once more to see his mother and the rest of the family. He and Jacob talked about going to England together, but Wilhelm returned to the front. Soon afterward he said goodbye to his father and simply walked away from the battlefield. He made his way to Hamburg and waited for Jacob to join him. A week or two later the two boys sailed for England.

Some accounts of William Herschel's life say that he was a deserter from the army and received a special pardon from King George III twenty-five years later. Actually, he received an official discharge, obtained for him by his father after he left. A copy of the certificate, signed by General Spörken and dated 1762, is preserved in the 1912 edition of *The Scientific Papers of Sir William Herschel.*

As soon as Wilhelm and Jacob arrived in London, some time in November 1757, they set out to find work. Fortunately they were not friendless in a strange land. On the contrary, both were welcomed by people they had met during their visit to England with the Hanoverian Guards. Wilhelm applied for work as a music copier and was assigned to copy an opera. He did that job so quickly and accurately that he was soon assured of a living from music manuscripts alone. For a while he supported Jacob, too, until the older brother found a place in an orchestra.

In 1759 Jacob went back to Hanover, assured of a violinist's chair in the court orchestra. Wilhelm remained in England, but the brothers kept in touch with each other. Their letters are still the main source of information about Wilhelm's early life in England.

After two years in London his transformation had begun. The former German oboist became more and more fluent in his new language and began to spell his name the English way. As *William* Herschel, he considered himself an Englishman.

In 1760, soon after Jacob left, William accepted an invitation from Lord Darlington, Colonel of the Durham Militia in Yorkshire, to come north as instructor to the militia band. He left London and traveled to Sunderland, where he became popular, successful, and thoroughly English.

With the same enthusiasm he brought to everything else he did, William Herschel not only trained the band musicians but composed special music to show them off to the best advantage. The band attracted the attention of music lovers for miles around, and so did its instructor. William soon found himself in demand as a private teacher and as a performer in the large country homes of Yorkshire. His work involved a lot of traveling—sometimes as much as fifty miles a day—so he bought a horse for making the rounds.

His letters to Jacob were full of lively accounts of his visits with various families. One letter told of his first personal encounter with royalty:

Now I must make you a little story about what I have done this week. My vanity has been a little flattered, for I had a message by a courier from Lady M. requesting my presence. I hastened thither and found at Halnaby the Duke of York, the King's brother. We made music for the whole week as his Royal Highness plays the violincello very well. I had the honour not only to play several solos with his approval but to be accompanied by him.

William's duets with the duke of York were not the end of his relationship with the royal family. Twenty years later, as an astronomer, he would be summoned by King George III, who would become his patron for the rest of his life.

Meanwhile, during the next five years Herschel moved around—in 1762 to a new job at Leeds, where he planned concerts and conducted the orchestra; then to Halifax, where he played the organ; finally, in 1766, to Bath, the fashionable English holiday town, where he was organist in a new church, called the Octagon Chapel because of its shape. Meanwhile, he continued to compose music—some of which can be heard on records today—and to give lessons to private pupils. Hostesses in Bath invited him to their homes as performer, teacher, and guest.

This schedule would have been full enough for most men, but William Herschel had many interests. He still found time to look at the stars, to learn Italian and classical Greek, and to study mathematics. His diary for 1766 contained several brief notes that had nothing to do with music. On February 19 he jotted down: "Wheatley. Observation of Venus." On February 24: "Eclipse of the moon at 7 o'clock A.M. Kirby." The same year he wrote to Jacob, "My leisure time was employed in reading mathematical books, such as the works of Emerson, Maclaurin, Hodgson, Smith's *Harmonics*, etc."

Soon after William moved to Bath, Jacob came to assist

his brother with the musical chores of the community. The following year, 1768, their twelve-year-old brother Dietrich was also sent to Bath, to study music with them. When their mother begged Dietrich to come home for his confirmation, Jacob took him back to Hanover. Jacob returned to Bath in 1770, accompanied by another brother, Alexander, then twenty-five, who liked Bath so much that he stayed there for fifty-six years.

Sophia, the older sister, had already married and left Hanover. Caroline, at home with her mother and Dietrich, felt left out and forgotten by her older brothers. Like Cinderella, she was confined to the kitchen when she wanted to be doing so many other things—learning languages, studying music, making a living as her brothers were doing. When Jacob came home to stay he offered her no encouragement. He seemed to agree with their mother that Caroline's place was at home, cooking, cleaning, and sewing for the family. Whenever she could, Caroline practiced her singing and prayed for a miracle to save her from a lifetime in a Hanover kitchen.

Sometime in 1771 a letter from William suggested that she come to Bath and take singing lessons. The offer seemed to be the miracle she had hoped for—but it wasn't. Jacob and her mother refused to let her go. In spite of their attitude Caroline began preparing for the trip, learning to sing the solo parts of violin concertos and knitting enough stockings for the family to keep it supplied after she was gone.

Finally, when his mother still refused to part with Caroline, William went to Hanover himself and brought her back to England. Caroline, then twenty-two, stayed with her brother for the rest of his life, serving as housekeeper, secretary, mechanic, and co-astronomer. In a way, she was also his biographer. Her memoirs contributed to history a detailed picture of the last fifty years of William Herschel's life.

By the time Caroline arrived in England, William was already devoting to astronomy and optics all the time he could spare from his busy musical schedule. Caroline's account of their trip from Hanover to Bath tells about an overnight stay in London: "In the evening, when the shops were lighted," she wrote, "we went to see all that was to be seen in that part of London; of which I remember only the optician shops, for I do not think we stopt at any other."

After they arrived in Bath, Caroline complained that she didn't see enough of her brother. His music kept him busy all day. At night,

in consequence of the harassing and fatiguing life he had led during the winter months, he used to retire to bed with a bason of milk or glass of water, and Smith's *Harmonics* and *Optics*, Ferguson's *Astronomy*, etc., and so went to sleep buried under his favourite authors; and his first thoughts on rising were how to obtain instruments for viewing those objects himself of which he had been reading.

William's growing preoccupation with stars and telescopes was reflected in the brief entries he made in his diary for 1773. On May 10 he noted: "Bought a book of astronomy and one of astronomical tables." On May 24: "Bought an object glass of 10 feet focal length." June 1: "Bought many eye glasses and tin tubes made." And on September 15: "Hired a 2 feet reflector."

Herschel had started his observations with refracting telescopes such as Kepler and Galileo had used. He soon discovered, as Newton had, that ordinary telescope lenses could not penetrate far enough into the sky to satisfy his curiosity about the stars. He bought ready-made lenses and tried building his own telescopes, increasing their power by mounting them in longer and longer tubes. After he tried to mount tin tubes that were 12 feet, 15 feet, and even 30 feet long, he found that these instruments were unsteady and unwieldy—not at all satisfactory for the kind of exploring Herschel wanted to do.

When he rented the little "2 feet reflector" mentioned in his diary, Herschel found it so much more manageable than the long tubes that he made up his mind to build a reflector of his own. He would make it a large one—at least twice as large as the one he had rented—because he wanted to penetrate deeper into the night sky, to see what stars existed beyond the ones other men had charted.

He knew that his telescope must serve two purposes: it must magnify the image of a star and also make it brighter. To make the image larger he needed a long tube, since the magnification of a telescope depends upon its focal length (the distance between the lens and the point where all rays of light meet at a single focus). He knew that a telescope of 10-foot focal length would double the size of an image seen through one of 5-foot focal length, using the same eyepiece. The diameter of the lens would make no difference in the magnification. So the long, skinny refracting telescopes he had made would magnify an image, but would do nothing to make it brighter.

The *brightness* of a star image seen through a telescope

depends upon the area of the objective lens or mirror. Herschel knew that if he doubled a mirror's diameter, he would gather four times as much light—because the *area* would be quadrupled. Therefore, a 6-inch mirror would show stars that were four times as faint as the faintest ones seen with a 3-inch mirror.

Herschel recognized this relationship between the aperture of a telescope, its light-gathering power, and its ability to penetrate deep into space. He became the first man to write about this relationship in a paper entitled *On the Power of Penetrating into Space by Telescopes,* which was published in 1799.

Even in 1774 he had made up his mind to build larger and larger telescopes. When he tried to find a large concave mirror with a focal length of about five feet, he had no luck. He was told that such a mirror could be custom-made for him, but the price would be appropriately astronomical. He knew what he wanted, so he decided to make his own mirror. He had never made any mirrors or lenses before, having depended upon the ready-made variety, but he didn't hesitate to try, especially after he heard that a set of optical tools could be bought in Bath. An elderly Quaker who was giving up his hobby of polishing mirrors was selling his equipment. Herschel seized the chance to buy the whole batch, along with some half-finished mirrors.

They were metal mirrors. In modern telescopes the mirrors are made of silvered glass, but in Herschel's time the process of silvering glass was unknown. Telescope makers used Newton's recipe for speculum (mirror) metal, sometimes experimenting with other combinations of metals. Herschel studied the reflecting powers of various metals and made up his own alloys. He melted the metals, poured them into molds, and ground and polished them himself, with the help of Alexander and Caroline.

By the spring of 1774 Herschel had mounted a mirror with a 5½-foot focal length, more than twice as powerful as the reflector he had rented. With this mirror he was able to observe the rings of Saturn and a "lucid spot in Orion's sword belt." This only whetted his appetite for more telescope making. Before long he was planning a 7-foot telescope with an aperture of 6.2 inches.

Everybody in the household was put to work. Pupils who came for music lessons found a cabinet maker in the drawing room, building tubes and stands. Their teacher sometimes rushed in from the kitchen with smudges of molten pitch on his clothes, taking time out from mixing alloys for his mirrors. Alexander had put up a huge machine in one of the bedrooms for grinding and turning eyepieces, and the sound of grinding often interrupted a concerto or sonata. Some of William's pupils became so fascinated by all the activity around them that they asked for lessons in astronomy as well as music.

In her memoirs Caroline recalled her housewifely misgivings when she "saw almost every room turned into a workshop." Her concern for her brother led her to nag him about eating and sleeping. William seemed to consider both a waste of time, but he sometimes allowed her to feed him, bite by bite, rather than interrupt the work his hands were doing.

. . . this was once the case [she wrote] when at the finishing of a 7 feet mirror he had not left his hands from it for 16 hours together. And in general he was never unemployed at meals, but always at the same time contriving or making drawings of whatever came into his mind. And generally I was obliged to read to him when at some work which required no thinking, and sometimes lending a hand, I became in time as useful a member of the workshop as a boy might be to his master in the first year of his apprenticeship.

Herschel later built telescopes that were twenty, thirty, and forty feet long, with apertures proportionately large, but the little 7-foot reflector, completed in 1775, remained his favorite. The following year he finished a 10-foot telescope and had a 20-foot giant mounted in the garden. In the middle of all this work he was offered the post of director of the Bath orchestra. He accepted.

When William was using his telescope curious neighbors often stopped by to ask questions, and he was always cordial about explaining his activities. One clear December night in 1779 he had set up his 7-foot treasure in the street outside his house and was observing the moon. On this particular night a passerby introduced himself as Dr. William Watson, a fellow of the Royal Society of London. After this brief introduction Dr. Watson became a regular visitor to the Herschel home and a close friend of William. Through him, William began to meet scientists for the first time, and he found them as congenial as musicians. A visit from the Astronomer Royal, Nevil Maskelyne, indicated that William Herschel, astronomer, was becoming as well known as William Herschel, musician.

Through Watson, William was invited to send scientific papers to the Royal Society. He responded by submitting thirty-one papers in 1780 and 1781 alone. It was faithful

Caroline Herschel kept meticulous records of her brother's astronomical observations and later became a noted astronomer.

Dr. Watson who spread the word when William made the discovery that won him international fame and completed, once and for all, his metamorphosis from musician to astronomer.

On March 13, 1781, Herschel was in his garden, sweeping the sky with his 7-foot favorite, cataloguing stars. Just inside the open door Caroline sat in the lamplight, taking notes as her brother called them out to her, thus saving his eyes from the strain of repeated adjustments from darkness to light. Between ten and eleven o'clock Herschel came across an object that didn't look like an ordinary star. "In the quartile near Zeta Tauri," he dictated to Caroline, "the lowest of two is a curious either nebulous star or perhaps a comet."

For four nights he watched the object and found that its position changed. It had a visible disc, like a planet, but all the known planets were accounted for; there were none in that location. Nobody had ever suggested that there might be undiscovered planets, beyond the six already known.

Herschel told Dr. Watson about the discovery and his friend immediately sent word to the Greenwich and Oxford observatories. Astronomers and mathematicians in England and on the continent were soon at work looking for the mysterious body, calculating its orbit, gradually becoming convinced that what Herschel had discovered was indeed a planet, invisible to the naked eye. Since the days of Galileo no discovery made with a telescope had created such a sensation.

Herschel named the planet *Georgium Sidus*, in honor of King George III, but many European astronomers objected to a name of English origin. All the other planets had names from Greek and Roman mythology. It seemed fitting that this far-off member of the sun's family should have a similar name. The German astronomer Johann Bode called it Uranus, the name that became permanent.

In May, within two months after he first sighted Uranus, Herschel was invited to London to meet Sir Joseph Banks, president of the Royal Society. In November he traveled again to London to receive the Copley Medal from the Society. In December that body elected him a fellow.

The demands of fame were not allowed to interrupt William Herschel's work. He was still teaching music, directing concerts, and making telescopes. Finally, in the summer of 1782, Herschel decided to give up his musical profession and devote all his time to astronomy. King George had offered him a pension of 200 pounds a year and had asked him to take a house near Windsor Castle, where the king could call for him from time to time. "In consequence of which," Herschel wrote, "I took a house at Datchet with a convenient garden in which my 20-feet reflector might be placed. I went then back to Bath to pack up my telescopes and furniture to be sent to Datchet, to which place I returned immediately."

After the move to Datchet he was busier than ever, filling orders for telescopes. The King ordered five 10-foot reflectors and other orders were pouring in. A list in William's handwriting mentions seventy-six telescopes made to fill orders from such luminaries as the king of Spain, the emperor of Austria, and Catharine the Great, empress of Russia, as well as assorted princes, dukes, and astronomers.

Meanwhile Herschel was planning to build the largest telescope the world had ever seen. It would have a mirror nearly forty-eight inches across, almost four times the size of his latest one. It was to be mounted in a huge cylinder, 40 feet long, to be supported by scaffolding that would tower above the trees in the garden. The Datchet garden was too small to accommodate such a monster, so William began to look for another house.

In the spring of 1786 the Herschels moved again—the last time for William—to a small red brick house with a spacious garden at Slough, within sight of Windsor. The house, later named Observatory House, stood as a memorial to Herschel and his discoveries until 1960, when it was pulled down.

King George, eager to finance the building of the world's greatest telescope, gave Herschel a grant of 2,000 pounds. The building of the giant telescope required five years and several attempts. The first metal disc was too thin. The second cracked while cooling. The third contained too much copper and was too dull. Finally, in February 1788, a successful casting was made of a 48-inch disc, three and a half inches thick and weighing more than a ton.

The precious disc was polished entirely by hand. Herschel hired two teams of workmen, twenty-four in all, to work in shifts around the clock. As if they were musicians, Herschel orchestrated their movements according to numbers painted on the backs of their overalls, then conducted them like a bandmaster.

Before the mammoth cylinder was mounted Herschel received another 2,000-pound grant from the King, plus an annual stipend for maintaining the telescope and an additional fifty pounds a year for Caroline, now officially recognized as his assistant.

Every detail of the enormous telescope was supervised by

Herschel himself. Yet he still swept the sky with his 20-foot telescope on every night that was clear enough for finding the double stars, nebulae, and clusters he was busily cataloguing. He even found time to get married, at the age of fifty, to Mary Pitt, an attractive widow who lived nearby.

A year after their wedding William and Mary Herschel celebrated the completion of the 40-foot telescope. The first time he looked through it, Herschel discovered two new moons of Saturn. (Five others had been discovered a century earlier by Christian Huygens and Giovanni Domenico Cassini.)

The telescope became one of the wonders of England, a tourist attraction that brought a stream of visitors into the Herschels' garden at Slough. They marveled at the huge leaning tube supported by scaffolding that was mounted on a wooden turntable. Herschel, always hospitable, escorted guests up a slightly shaky ladder to a wooden cage suspended from the tube near the eyepiece. Once inside the cage, the observer could be raised or lowered or turned in a circle with the tube while Herschel lectured on the wonders to be seen through the eyepiece.

Scientists, musicians, neighbors, casual visitors—all were charmed by Herschel's enthusiasm and good humor. A visiting Swiss professor wrote, "Visitors often take unwarranted advantage of his courtesy and compliance, wasting time and putting unnecessary and often ridiculous questions, but his patience is inexhaustible and he takes these inconveniences . . . in such good part that no one could guess how much they cost him."

One female guest called Herschel "a delightful man, extremely modest for all his vast knowledge; candid as a child,

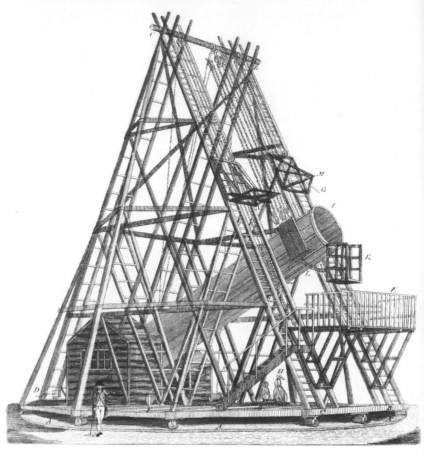

Herschel's 40-foot reflector and his good-humored hospitality attracted crowds of visitors to his garden observatory at Slough.

delicately tactful and considerate . . . . life seems a perfect joy to him. There is no happier man in all England."

He and Mary had still another reason to be happy on March 7, 1792, when their son was born. They named him John Frederick William Herschel, and his name would take its place with his father's in the history of science.

When John was born William was fifty-four. He had already lived a full, successful life—devoted to "the pursuit of knowledge" according to his boyhood vow—and he had thirty more active, productive years ahead. He would live to see his son recognized as a distinguished astronomer and telescope maker.

While John was growing up William completed some of his most significant work among the stars that lay beyond the solar system—and beyond the Milky Way. His studies of the motions of double stars led him to the conclusion that they are held together by gravitational force and revolve about a common center. He catalogued more than eight hundred such pairs.

Herschel's studies of the blurry patches of light called *nebulae* (from the Latin word for cloud or mist) started a new kind of star research that laid the foundation for modern astrophysics. He was the first astronomer to suggest that nebulae might be distant galaxies, far beyond the Milky Way.

During his early studies Herschel assumed that all nebulae were clusters of individual stars, too far away to be seen individually by his telescopes. Later he proposed that there might be two kinds of nebulae—some made of stars and others partly composed of "a shining fluid of a nature totally unknown to us." This fluid, he believed, condensed into solid bodies—stars. By 1811 his hypothesis had become more specific, describing a sort of chain reaction, set off by gravitational pull, that resulted in the compression of the mysterious "shining fluid" into solid star forms.

The question of the origin of stars continued to puzzle astronomers for more than a century after Herschel's death, but his hypothesis marked a path to be followed by the new astrophysicists. Astronomers of the 1890's, with the help of more powerful telescopes than were available to Herschel, discovered that he was not entirely right about all the details, but that his imagination had led him in the right direction. Some so-called nebulae were indeed distant galaxies, made up of innumerable stars. Others seemed to be masses of hot gas, rather than "fluid," as Herschel had supposed. His hypothesis served as a working basis for a century of research, which in the late 1930's led to modern theories of stellar evolution, based on knowledge of nuclear energy.

William Herschel was the first astronomer to suggest that the solar system is moving through space. The Copernicans had been convinced that the sun stood still, but Herschel discovered that it moved, carrying with it the whole system of planets and moons. He even indicated a point in the heavens from which he believed it to be moving. Modern cosmologists believe that our whole galaxy—the Milky Way—is moving out and away from other galaxies in an expanding universe.

In 1816 at the age of seventy-eight the venerable astronomer became *Sir* William Herschel, knighted by the Prince Regent. Four years later, when the Royal Astronomical Society was founded, Herschel was persuaded to accept the presidency, though he was too ill and weak by that time to attend meetings. His son, just out of Cambridge, was a member of the society and served on the committee to draft a constitution. Twenty-two years later John Herschel would become president of the society.

William Herschel did his final work as a telescope maker in 1820. He was too feeble to do the actual grinding, figuring, and polishing himself, but he supervised and directed while John did the work. The result of this father-and-son collaboration was a 20-foot telescope that John set up later at the Cape of Good Hope. He used it to map the skies above the southern hemisphere as his father had done in the north.

On August 15, 1822, Caroline Herschel went to the spot in the garden where she usually found her brother. Every morning she read the newspaper to him, since his eyes had grown weak. That day, she found that he had gone back to his room and she went up to see how he was feeling. As soon as he saw her, he sent her to the library to bring one of his latest papers on the Milky Way. When she returned with the paper she found him being put to bed by Mary and the housekeeper, too weak to support himself. Ten days later, on August 25, he died at the age of eighty-four.

5

JOSEPH VON FRAUNHOFER'S
LINES AND LENSES

Joseph von Fraunhofer's telescope lenses were virtually flawless, the most nearly perfect ones the world had ever seen.
Before 1820, when Herschel's 40-foot reflector was still at-
tracting crowds to his garden at Slough, this young Bavarian
optician was at work on a refractor that would become a
model for the finest modern astronomical telescopes. Not
only was the 9½-inch lens completely free of distortions and
colored fringes, but the turntable on which it was mounted
solved a nonoptical problem that had always bothered
astronomers:

Since the earth turns in one direction and the sky seems
to move in the opposite direction, how can an observer keep
his telescope focused on a particular star without frequent
stops to adjust the position of the instrument? If the telescope weighs several tons, the problem is serious.

Fraunhofer eliminated this difficulty for astronomers who
used his telescopes by designing a turntable that was balanced on ball bearings and driven by clockwork. It allowed
his telescope to move against the motion of the earth, ex-

Joseph von Fraunhofer (1787–1826).

actly as the sky seemed to move, so that a given star could be kept in sight all night without interruption.

The inventor of the clockwork turntable and other ingenious tools of astronomy was born on March 6, 1787, at Straubing, Bavaria. His father, Franz Xavier Fraunhofer, was a master glazier. Young Joseph began to learn about glassworking almost as soon as he could walk and talk. His mother died when he was eleven and the following year he lost his father. An older sister, Anna Theresa, took care of Joseph for a while, but she was unable to run their father's business. When the business was sold, it brought so little money that Anna had to make arrangements for Joseph to support himself.

About 1800 he was sent to Munich to be apprenticed to a glass polisher and mirror maker, Philipp Anton Weichselberger. As an apprentice Joseph made no money, but at least he had a place to live with the Weichselbergers and shared their food. His schooling had been cut short when he came to Munich, but he was learning everything Weichselberger could teach him about mirrors and glass.

Joseph Fraunhofer might have spent his life making mirrors, if a near-fatal accident had not brought him a lucky chance to continue his education. The Weichselbergers had their home and shop in a building that was so old and run-down that neighbors often wondered why it didn't collapse. On July 21, 1801, it did just that. The crumbling walls caved in without warning, burying everyone inside under the debris. Frau Weichselberger and several others were killed. Fourteen-year-old Joseph was pulled from the ruins with broken bones and bleeding wounds, but he was alive.

At the hospital, soon after he regained consciousness,

Joseph was visited by the elector of Bavaria, a prince with a social conscience. Just after the Weichselbergers' house had collapsed, the prince had gone to investigate conditions in the slum neighborhood and had been told about the orphan boy who survived the accident. He went to see the boy, talked with him for a while, and was impressed by his quick intelligence and his interest in optics. Before leaving the hospital, the elector promised Joseph a sum of money to allow him to resume his education. A few days later young Fraunhofer received a package of books on optics—a gift from the elector.

When he left the hospital and went back to work, Joseph was determined to continue his education. In those days Munich had no public schools for boys his age, but a local priest, Father Xavier Kefer, had set up a private school where working boys could attend classes in the evenings and on weekends. Joseph Fraunhofer became one of Father Kefer's most enthusiastic pupils.

Three years later, at seventeen, Fraunhofer joined the staff of Utzschneider and Reichenbach, an optical firm in a suburb of Munich. He was the youngest journeyman in the company but obviously knowledgeable about glass and lenses, and eager to learn more. He was particularly eager to learn from Pierre Louis Guinand, a senior staff member who had come to Munich from Switzerland. Guinand's glass discs were sought by lens makers as the clearest and purest in Europe.

Guinand, formerly a cabinet maker in his native Neuchâtel, had become interested in telescopes about thirty-five years earlier when he had borrowed one from a friend. It was a small reflecting telescope and seemed simple enough to copy. He took it apart to study it, then built one of his own, casting and polishing the metal mirror himself. Later, experimenting with refracting telescopes, he was troubled by the bubbles that were always present in the glass discs he bought to grind into lenses. He tried to make his own glass and discovered where the bubbles came from.

In its molten state the glass had to be stirred, and there seemed to be no way to avoid stirring in enough air to make bubbles. Guinand had used a wooden stick for stirring, as other glassmakers did, but he wondered what would happen if he tried some other material. When he stirred the next batch of molten glass with a fired-clay stirring rod, he found that the bubbles rose quickly to the surface and the glass cooled with fewer flaws.

Fraunhofer was fascinated by Guinand's work and full of questions. The older man was flattered at first and made Fraunhofer his assistant, but he was annoyed when his teen-age helper began to make suggestions for improving his methods. Guinand's lenses were the best Fraunhofer had ever seen, but he felt there was room for improvement. He was constantly experimenting with Guinand's furnace— changing the direction of the flame, trying new spouts, lengthening or shortening the vent. What irritated Guinand even more was the success of his assistant's experiments. Young Fraunhofer was too often right.

While Joseph Fraunhofer was antagonizing Guinand with his constant tampering, he was making a study of all kinds of optical glass. He wanted to find out what caused various defects, then find a way to correct them. His goal was to produce the perfect telescope lens.

Earlier optical researchers had made some progress since

the days when young Isaac Newton complained that the rainbow-fringed images he saw through his telescope gave him a headache. Newton had concluded that there was no way to get rid of these colored blurs because it was impossible to bend light through a lens without splitting it up into the colors of the spectrum. So he built a reflecting telescope that used a mirror to get around the problem.

Other experimenters continued to try to produce lenses that would show color-free images. One of these was John Dollond, an English silk weaver who became interested in lenses and read Newton's *Opticks*. About twenty years after Newton's death Dollond produced a lens which almost eliminated the colored distortions. It was a compound lens made of two kinds of glass—a convex lens of crown glass fitted into a concave lens of flint glass. Each lens used by itself would focus various colors of light at different points, causing a blurred image. Furthermore, the arrangement of varying focal points was different in each lens. But by combining the two kinds of lenses, Dollond was able to bring light of all colors together at a single focus, producing a sharp, color-free image.

By 1752 Dollond's workshop in London was manufacturing the best lenses known, but they still had flaws. It was next to impossible to make a batch of glass that was exactly like any other batch. Even the best discs had bubbles and streaks until Guinand discovered the secret of the fired-clay stirring rod that reduced the number of bubbles.

When Joseph Fraunhofer set out to improve Guinand's lenses, he was trying to surpass the superbly refined product of a century of research since the first publication of Newton's *Opticks* in 1704.

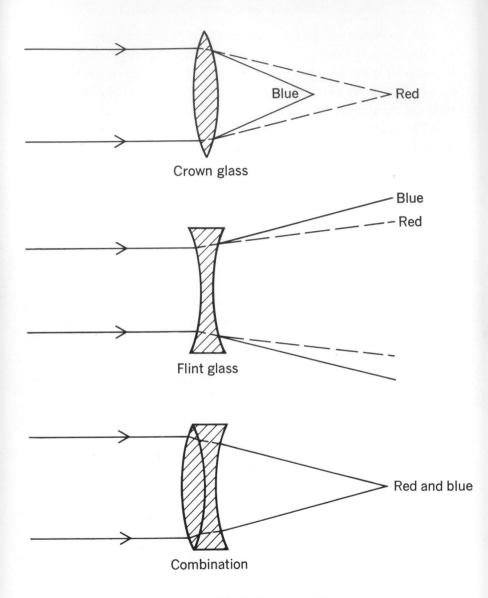

Crown glass

Flint glass

Combination

Dollond's Compound Lens

110

Fraunhofer set a task for himself—to find out exactly how much each color of the spectrum is bent by each kind of glass. In the course of his experiments he set up a telescope with a prism in front of it to catch and break up into its component colors the sunlight admitted through a slit in a window shade. It was the first spectroscope—though it was not given this name until much later—and it became an indispensable tool of modern astrophysics.

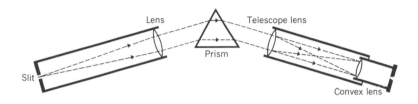

Fraunhofer's Spectroscope

While examining the spectrum spread out by the prism, Fraunhofer made an unexpected discovery. As he described it later: "I saw with the telescope an almost countless number of strong and weak vertical lines which are darker than the rest of the color image. Some appeared perfectly black." At first he thought the lines might be produced by a flaw in the prism or telescope lens, but repeated experiments convinced him that they were characteristic of the light itself. "I have convinced myself," he wrote, "by means of various experiments and by varying the methods that these lines and bands are due to the nature of sunlight and do not arise from diffraction, illusion, etc."

These lines in the spectrum had been noticed before by an English scientist, William Hyde Wollaston, who published a paper about them in 1802. He thought the lines were boundaries between the various colors of the spectrum. Some lines seemed a little blurred, but Wollaston assumed that the flaw was in the human eye. Other lines were obviously not boundaries, but these, Wollaston said, "I cannot undertake to explain."

Without knowing about Wollaston's theory—which was wrong anyway—Fraunhofer *did* undertake to explain all the lines. After examining the spectrum of direct sunlight, Fraunhofer turned his rudimentary spectroscope toward the moon and found: "The light of the moon gave me a spectrum which showed in the brightest colors the same fixed lines as did sunlight, and in exactly the same places." When he looked at Venus and Mars, he identified the very same lines. Were they characteristic of *all* light, from any source?

So far Fraunhofer had tested only sunlight. The light of the moon and planets was, after all, merely reflected from the sun. Now he pointed his telescope toward the stars. Again, in each spectrum he found lines—but not the same lines. Their position and intensity were different from those in the spectrum of sunlight. Each star had its own distinctive spectrum. Some closely resembled others, but there were variations that made each star distinguishable from other stars by the lines in its spectrum. Fraunhofer charted the lines and identified each line by a letter or by a combination of letters and numbers. He was not sure what the lines meant but he continued to study them.

As for the original purpose of his experiments—to mea-

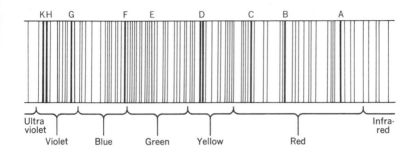

Fraunhofer Lines

sure precisely the optical qualities of various kinds of glass —Fraunhofer thought he had failed. "It would be most advantageous," he wrote, "if one could measure for every kind of glass the dispersion for every color, but the different colors in the spectrum have no definite limits, and so this cannot be determined immediately from the color image. The uncertainty is so great that the experiment is useless."

He was right about the uncertainty, but wrong when he said the experiment was useless. The lines he had discovered—still known as *Fraunhofer lines*—became the key to a mystery that had been considered unsolvable. Fraunhofer puzzled over the lines for the rest of his life. He never understood their significance, but thirty years after his death another German physicist discovered that Fraunhofer lines were clues to the types of substances from which the various colors came. These lines would reveal to scientists the chemical makeup of the stars.

Even though Joseph Fraunhofer could not explain the lines, he sensed that they were a discovery worth reporting. He referred to them in 1814 in a paper submitted to the Munich Academy of Sciences: *Determination of the Refractive and Dispersive Power of Different Kinds of Glass with Reference to the Perfecting of Achromatic Telescopes.* This paper, describing his attempts to measure the dispersion of each color in the spectrum, was published by the academy in 1817.

Soon afterward Fraunhofer was elected a member of the Munich Academy, a rare honor for a man whose occupation was then considered technology rather than science. But if any members of the academy had doubts about Joseph Fraunhofer's qualifications as a scientist, they were soon convinced that the man was much more than a mere lens grinder. After continuing and expanding his studies of the mysterious lines in the spectrum, he submitted another paper, entitled *New Modification of Light by the Mutual Influence and Diffraction of the Rays and the Laws of this Modification.* This paper described in detail his discoveries and charted more than five hundred spectrum lines. It was published by the academy in 1821 and read by physicists all over the world—then and long afterward, even today.

During the years when Fraunhofer was contributing his ideas and discoveries to pure science, he was also providing some very practical and concrete tools for astronomers. His telescope lenses were so much better than those produced by his teacher Guinand that the older man resigned from his position at the optical company and went to France.

By the time he was twenty-five Fraunhofer was in charge of forty-eight workmen at Utzschneider and Reichenbach. A few years later, when the optical branch of the company split off from the instrument factory, it became Utzschneider and Fraunhofer. The young man was a full partner and his name was becoming a synonym for fine telescopes. To own a "Fraunhofer" was to own the best telescope money could buy.

In 1820 Fraunhofer completed his masterpiece, a refracting telescope with a flawless 9½-inch lens. It became famous as the Dorpat refractor, acclaimed by astronomers as the finest refracting telescope in the world at the time. Sky observers who had abandoned lens telescopes in favor of mirror telescopes began to reconsider.

William Herschel had shown what could be done with large reflectors. Each time he doubled the diameter of a mirror, he quadrupled the amount of light gathered into his telescope, producing brighter images of distant objects. A larger lens likewise gathers more light than a smaller lens, but it was a lot easier to make a large mirror than a large lens. For one thing, a mirror could be made of thin metal. Only the reflecting surface is involved in bouncing light rays to a focus. But a refracting telescope depends upon the whole lens—both surfaces and all the glass in between. Light passes *through* the lens and is bent toward a focus on the other side. A convex telescope lens with a large light-gathering area would be thick and heavy, requiring flawless glass to produce undistorted images and special supports to keep it stable.

In Fraunhofer's time many astronomers used large mirrors to gather more light, but they discovered disadvantages. Metal mirrors inevitably tarnished when exposed to air. A great deal of time, skill, and precision were required to re-polish the surface—and the job had to be done often. Astronomers who preferred refractors argued that they required less upkeep and produced sharper images, especially since Dollond and Fraunhofer had virtually eliminated the problem of colored haze.

Fraunhofer's 9½-inch refracting telescope had been ordered by Friedrich Georg Wilhelm Struve, a German-born astronomer who was now in charge of a new observatory at Dorpat, Estonia. It was for this telescope that Fraunhofer designed his perfectly balanced turntable on ball bearings, completely different from any mounting used before. His ingenious clockwork motor made the telescope follow the stars, compensating for the rotation of the earth. Graduated circles around the mounting made it easier for observers to read angles and pinpoint the location of stars.

With Fraunhofer's Dorpat refractor Struve catalogued more than two thousand double stars. Struve's three books on the subject are still standard references for astronomers. When in 1839 Czar Nicholas I of Russia appointed Struve director of the new Pulkovo Observatory near Leningrad, the astronomer immediately ordered another Fraunhofer refractor. By this time the great telescope maker was dead, but his successor supervised the building of a new 15-inch refractor, built acccording to Fraunhofer's design.

While the Dorpat telescope was making its first surveys in 1823, Fraunhofer was appointed head of the Optical and Physical Institute at Munich. That same year, in France, the philosopher Auguste Comte wrote that there was one secret

Russia's Pulkovo observatory, near Leningrad, ordered a fifteen-inch lens. Fraunhofer died before finishing it.

the scientists, for all their learning, could never solve. Man could never know, he said, what the stars were made of. Comte did not know that Joseph Fraunhofer had already found the key to this mystery. The lines he had charted in the spectrum would provide the answer.

Fraunhofer did not live to see the secrets unlocked by his discovery. He died of tuberculosis on June 7, 1826, while preparing for a vacation in Italy. He was only thirty-nine.

Thirty-three years later, in the Heidelberg laboratory of Robert Bunsen, inventor of the Bunsen burner, Gustav Robert Kirchhoff was studying luminous gases. While experimenting with vaporized sodium, the physicist studied it through a spectroscope and noticed two bright lines in the spectrum. Checking Fraunhofer's chart of the dark lines he had found in sunlight, Kirchhoff discovered that his two bright lines were in exactly the same place as the dark ones marked D_1 and D_2 on the chart. When he allowed sunlight to shine through the sodium flame, he was astonished to see the dark D lines appear in place of the bright ones. The bright lines in the spectrum, he concluded, had something to do with the presence of sodium.

Experimenting further, Kirchhoff found that a hydrogen flame in sunlight produced a line corresponding to the F line on Fraunhofer's chart. Oxygen produced an A line and iron an E line. These lines in the sun's spectrum were a coded message, revealing the chemical makeup of the sun. Before he was through Kirchhoff had discovered that the sun contained such familiar elements as sodium, magnesium, iron, calcium, copper, and zinc. With Fraunhofer lines, astronomers would be able to decode the chemical composition of the universe.

While Fraunhofer's inventions and discoveries were leading chemists, physicists, and astronomers into a new kind of teamwork, the world's great observatories were using his telescopes to map the sky. Fraunhofer's refractors were the favored instruments of leading astronomers, but Herschel's giant reflectors were not entirely forgotten. In Ireland a wealthy landowner was at work on a gigantic telescope that would make Herschel's 40-foot wonder look like a dwarf.

6

LORD ROSSE'S LEVIATHAN
OF PARSONSTOWN

The *Proceedings of the Royal Irish Academy* for 1840 reported: "Lord Oxmantown is about to construct a telescope of unequaled dimensions." It was to have a mirror six feet in diameter, mounted in a tube more than fifty feet long. Such a telescope would be able to look far beyond the most distant star clusters and nebulae catalogued by Sir William Herschel and his son. Perhaps it could tell astronomers what these nebulae were made of.

Five years later the telescope was completed and mounted in the park of Birr Castle near Parsonstown, Ireland, a low damp region near the Bog of Allen. It became known as "The Leviathan of Parsonstown," the world's largest telescope at that time, with the biggest metal mirror ever cast.

From a distance it looked like the top of a fortress with turrets defended by a gigantic cannon. The tube of the telescope, 54 feet long and 6 feet across, was big enough for a double column of soldiers to march through without bumping their heads. To protect it from the wind the telescope had been mounted between two stone walls built in medi-

William Parsons, Third Earl of Rosse (1800–1867).

eval style to blend with the castle. The highly polished metal mirror alone weighed four tons and the mounting contained more than one hundred and fifty tons of cast iron, along with other materials.

Who was the "Lord Oxmantown" who had designed the telescope, paid for it, and supervised its construction? By the time the instrument was mounted in 1845 he had become the Third Earl of Rosse, master of Birr Castle, and an Irish representative in the British Parliament. "Oxmantown" had been a temporary title acquired in 1821, when, as a student at Oxford, he had been elected to represent the university in the House of Commons.

He was born William Parsons, son of Lawrence Parsons, Second Earl of Rosse, on June 17, 1800, the year a reluctant Ireland had been united with England under a single government. As a child William learned from his father that the earls of Rosse were fiercely loyal to Ireland. Their Parsons ancestors had been English, two centuries earlier, but the Parsons men had married women of ancient Irish families, and their descendants shared the double heritage of England and Ireland.

William's father boasted that an earlier Lawrence Parsons, for whom he was named, had been sentenced to death in 1689 for rebellion against the king of England—but the execution was called off in the nick of time.

In the family library at Birr Castle young William found volumes of Irish poetry in the original Gaelic. His father read them aloud, savoring the strange musical sound of the language. If William would learn Gaelic, the earl said, he could discover for himself the story of Ireland, the ancient land that flourished long before the English came to the island. On one library shelf William found a small leather-bound book, in English, *A Defense of the Ancient History of Ireland*, by Lawrence Parsons, Second Earl of Rosse. Reading it, William began to understand the intensity of his father's affection for his country.

When he was eighteen, William entered Trinity College in Dublin, knowing that his career had been chosen for him. Some day he would have to take over his father's seat in the House of Lords as well as the feudal estate at Parsonstown. While William pursued his studies his father was trying to make himself heard in Parliament, seeking some measure of justice for the Catholics in Ireland.

The earl of Rosse was Protestant; otherwise he would not have had the right to speak. For more than a hundred years, under the Penal Laws, Irish Catholics had been denied fundamental rights that are now taken for granted. They could not vote, own land, manufacture goods for export, or enter Trinity College in Dublin.

Surrounded by other Irish students, all of them Protestant, William was disturbed by the unfairness of his advantage. Suppose he had been born to one of the tenant families on his father's Parsonstown estate? What kind of life could he hope for? His father had set up schools for the children of tenants, but other landlords were not so considerate. What if he had been born to Catholic tenants of some other landlord's estate? Even if he had managed to learn to read, where could he have gone to borrow books?

The bothersome questions followed William when he left Dublin to enter Magdalen College at Oxford in 1821. That same year, when he was twenty-one, he was elected to represent the school in Parliament as Lord Oxmantown.

Now he had a platform from which he could plead for fair treatment of all Irishmen. Before William gave up his seat in the House of Commons, the Irish leader Daniel O'Connell had won emancipation, at least in name, for the Catholics of Ireland.

Meanwhile, the young Lord Oxmantown had discovered a new interest. His classes in astronomy had introduced him to the stars and he knew that he wanted to learn more about the unexplored heavens. When he read the works of Isaac Newton his imagination was stirred by the problems of optics. The more he read about Newton's reflecting telescope and the later, larger ones built by the Herschels, the more eager he became to build a large telescope of his own.

When he left Oxford William Parsons returned to his ancestral castle with a plan that combined his most cherished ambitions. He was going to build a telescope, study the stars, and help the children of his father's tenants educate themselves to look beyond the plowed furrows of Parsonstown. There were many bright young men living on the estate who might learn to be chemists, metallurgists, engineers, or opticians—if they had the chance. William intended to provide books and teachers for them. Later he would put them to work mixing alloys, casting metal, polishing mirrors, mounting his telescope. It couldn't be done overnight, but William was patient.

From time to time, as Lord Oxmantown, William still traveled to England to sit in the House of Commons. At the same time he continued to study astronomy, visiting observatories and planning the telescope he wanted to build. At the Armagh Observatory in Ireland he met the director, the Reverend Thomas Romney Robinson, an astronomer-priest whose father, a Protestant archbishop, had founded the observatory and library.

Dr. Robinson took an interest in William's plan for erecting the telescope and for training the men who would help him build it. William told him about a polishing machine he had designed to be driven by a steam engine. The priest encouraged him to write an article about the machine for the *Edinburgh Journal of Science*. The article appeared in 1828, the first of many William was to write for the journal.

Meanwhile, as a fellow of the Royal Society and a member of the Royal Irish Academy, Dr. Robinson was telling other prominent scientists about the work of the energetic young Lord Oxmantown. He offered to work with William on his project and collaborated with him on several papers for the Royal Irish Academy.

Early in 1830 the *Edinburgh Journal* published an "Account of a Series of Experiments on the Construction of Large Reflecting Telescopes," by "The Rt. Hon. Lord Oxmantown, M.P., etc." The article did not pretend to be a success story. On the contrary, it described unsuccessful experiments and disappointments—the mirrors that cracked or spotted, the alloys that were too brittle or adversely affected by atmospheric changes.

In making these experiments [William wrote] I have had two objects in view: *first*, to ascertain whether it was practicable to remove any of the defects known to exist in the large reflecting telescopes hitherto constructed; and *secondly*, to simplify the process necessary for the manufacture of good reflecting telescopes of ordinary dimensions, so that the art might be no longer a mystery, known to but few individuals, and not to be acquired, but after many years of laborious apprenticeship.

The author told how he had succeeded in removing some of the defects in his mirrors and set down in careful detail the procedures he had followed, so that others might test his methods for themselves. He described his failures, urging other telescope makers not to become discouraged if mirrors cracked or turned yellow.

It is well known [he wrote] that Sir William Herschel, at the commencement of his career, polished 400 specula of different dimensions; content if he could procure one tolerably good one out of that great number. Such were the difficulties that he had to encounter; and I am not aware that anything has been published since that time, tending materially to diminish the labours of the experimentalist, or of the practical optician.

Lord Oxmantown was eager to share his formula for making a particularly brilliant alloy and his method for making a "crack-proof" large mirror. To strengthen the mirror he first prepared a strong base of copper and zinc. Then he applied his rather brittle but brilliant speculum metal in thin wedge-shaped sections, like pieces of pie, and fused them to the base with tin. By gradually raising the temperature to melt the tin, applying pressure, then reducing the temperature again, he obtained a mirror "composed of zinc and copper, plated with speculum metal one quarter of an inch thick, adhering to it as firmly in every part as if it had been one piece of metal." The whole process was illustrated with diagrams.

By 1834 Lord Oxmantown was much too busy with his telescope making to interrupt his work with trips to England, so he resigned his seat in the House of Commons. He wanted to devote most of his time to astronomy—and to his training program for the young men of Parsonstown—while he was still free of other responsibilities. He knew that his father would be too old, in a few years, to remain active as a member of Parliament and master of Birr Castle.

After five more years of patient trial and error William had cast, polished, and mounted a successful 3-foot mirror in a telescope almost exactly like Herschel's garden giant at Slough, although not so large. The *Edinburgh Journal* published a sketch of the instrument, set among its ladders, scaffolding and pulleys, with Lord Oxmantown in a top hat standing stiffly on a platform near the eyepiece.

Once the telescope was mounted William and his colleague, Dr. Robinson, began to study some of the 2,500 nebulae catalogued by the Herschels. They hoped to prove William Herschel's theory that these misty blurs in the sky were made up of millions and billions of individual stars, too far away to be resolved into separate points of light by any existing telescope.

William's 3-foot reflector was a superior instrument but it was not powerful enough to show separate stars—if there were separate stars—in distant nebulae. He reported his observations to the Royal Society in London and made up his mind to build a larger telescope. He would make it twice as large—with a 6-foot mirror—the largest telescope the world had ever seen. Dr. Robinson was enthusiastic about the plan and couldn't wait to report it to the Royal Irish Academy. The scientific world was talking about the telescope long before the mirror was ready to be cast.

In 1840 the project was begun. Special furnaces were designed for melting the metal, cranes were raised to lift the crucibles, a 6-foot ring mold was set in a sand pit to shape the disc for the mirror, and a special railroad was laid to carry the disc to the annealing oven, where it would be heated, then slowly cooled to make it less brittle. Since there was no oven big enough for a 6-foot slab of metal, a new one had to be built. All the work was done by skilled workmen and specialists from Parsonstown whose training had been made possible by William Parsons.

Suddenly, in 1841 Sir Lawrence Parsons died and William became the Third Earl of Rosse. The new title made little difference at first in the routine of his life. He continued to supervise the workshops and building sites where preparations were being made for the telescope. Often he put on overalls and went to work beside the men he had trained. On rare nights when the sky was clear, he made observations with his 3-foot telescope. He wrote papers for the British Association for the Advancement of Science and was elected president of that group in 1843. Soon afterward he became a fellow of the distinguished Royal Society. Confident that his new telescope would provide the answers to many unanswered questions, he hinted to his fellow astronomers that new revelations would soon be made.

"There can be little doubt," he wrote, "but that discoveries will multiply in proportion as the telescope may be improved. It is perhaps not too much to expect that the time is not far distant when data will be collected sufficient to afford us some insight into the construction of the material universe." While trying to find this insight with his telescope, he was unaware that Fraunhofer had already

Lord Rosse's giant telescope was protected by fortresslike walls.

found the key to a different kind of insight with his dark lines in the spectrum. But in the 1840's Kirchhoff's discovery of the chemical significance of these lines was still in the future.

In 1844, after nearly four years of preparation, Lord Rosse was ready to cast his huge mirror. The three furnaces were stoked with Irish peat and started burning. Four tons of metal were shoveled into the crucibles. Once the metal had been melted, poured into the mold, and cooled, it was hoisted aboard a railroad car for the trip to the oven. Once out of the oven, the disc was allowed to cool for sixteen weeks before polishing could begin. Then the steam engines were fired and the polishing wheels set in motion.

Even before the mirror was polished the mounting was being constructed. One of the most difficult problems was to provide a stable foundation for this heavy unwieldy in-

129

strument. Lord Rosse solved the problem by designing a platform of 27 cast iron plates on a base of tree trunks. The whole thing rested on a ball and socket set into solid rock. Then the fortress-like walls were raised to shield the telescope on two sides.

Almost as soon as the great telescope was mounted and ready to be used for observations, the new earl of Rosse was called away from Birr Castle. He had been impatient to resume his studies of nebulae but had to postpone them to take his seat in the House of Lords. As it happened, the postponement lasted three years. Ireland faced one of the most tragic chapters in human history. All the Irish representatives rushed to London to beg the British Parliament for help.

At that time, in almost every part of Ireland the people lived on potatoes. If the farmers grew anything else they exported it to make money to pay their rent to the landlords. Potatoes were the mainstay of their diet and their economy. If a potato crop were to fail, millions of Irish farmers would face starvation. But there had been plenty of potatoes for several years and the harvest of 1845 promised to be the biggest ever. Then the time came to dig the potatoes from the ground and the farmers discovered the disaster—a blight had destroyed most of the crop.

The following year another crop was blighted, and famine spread. Within three years a million Irish people had died of starvation and disease. Another million left the country, many of them emigrating to Canada and the United States.

During the famine, few people in Ireland had time to wonder what was being done with the gigantic telescope in the park at Birr Castle. But the world's astronomers had been waiting for its completion. Now they demanded to know what observations were being made. There were rumors that it was a great "white elephant," poorly mounted and useless. Obviously it could not be used to sweep the sky as Herschel's telescopes had done. It was aimed at the south and could not be swung around to any other direction. Its view was limited to the strip of sky that passed over it.

The British Astronomer Royal, Sir George Airy, was impatient. Observers in Berlin, probing the sky with one of Fraunhofer's relatively small refractors, had found a new planet, Neptune. Its existence and location beyond Uranus had been predicted, almost simultaneously, by a British student, John Couch Adams, and a French mathematician, Urbain Jean-Joseph Leverrier. Neither man had access to a telescope powerful enough to prove his calculations.

When news of the planet came from the Berlin Observatory, Leverrier was given credit for the mathematical discovery of Neptune. Sir George protested indignantly that the earlier discovery was British and that the credit should go to Adams. Why, he wanted to know, had the planet not been detected first by Lord Rosse's super-telescope, the world's largest? Lord Rosse, still pleading for relief for his starving countrymen, had more immediate problems on his mind.

The Reverend Dr. Robinson, feeling that Lord Rosse's critics should be answered, published a statement in the March 1848 *Proceedings of the Royal Irish Academy:*

He has often been asked why this instrument has given no further results [Dr. Robinson wrote]. They who put the question had but a faint idea of the overwhelming pressure which the last three years exerted here on all who were resolved to discharge the duties which men owe their country. Lord Rosse is not a person to seek knowledge or enjoyment in the heavens when he ought to be employed on earth; and he devoted all his energy to relieve the present misery and provide for the future. . . . These days of evil are past . . . .

They were not over, but the situation had improved. Lord Rosse and his Irish colleagues had obtained loans through Parliament that would help to treat the sick and feed some of the hungry people of Ireland. In the summer of 1848 Lord Rosse was able to return to Birr Castle. He invited the Astronomer Royal to come for a visit and use the great telescope.

Sir George Airy accepted the invitation but considered the visit a waste of time because of the foggy weather. In letters to his wife he described the Irish nights as "vexatious," "hopeless," and "absolutely repulsive."

Lord Rosse, more accustomed to the "repulsive" climate, managed to make good use of the few clear nights that came along. Over the next fifteen years he made systematic studies of the nebulae that fascinated him, opening up new paths of discovery that are still being followed.

At that time astronomers applied the Latin term *nebula* (cloud) to all kinds of diffuse luminous areas in the sky, not knowing that some were *galaxies*, like our own, made up of millions and billions of stars, and that others, like the bright nebula in Orion, were merely luminous masses of dust and gas.

The master of Birr Castle was disappointed that his new telescope was not able to resolve many nebulae into separate stars, as he had hoped, but his findings led later astronomers to distinguish between various kinds of nebulae and galaxies. Meanwhile Lord Rosse contributed drawings of the nebulae he could see most clearly. He revealed, for the first time, the characteristic spiral shape of many of them.

There were times when even a loyal Irishman had to admit that the undependable climate was a handicap to an astronomer. During weeks of fog and rain when his work was interrupted, Lord Rosse corresponded with other astronomers—especially at Cambridge, in the United States, and at Pulkovo in Russia—urging them to join him in studying the nebulae.

As his fame grew Lord Rosse was called away from his telescope more and more often. He was named president of the Royal Society and was asked to make speeches at gatherings of scientists. In 1862 he was named chancellor of the University of Dublin, where he spent the final five years of his life. But his telescope was still being used for observations at Birr Castle, under the direction of his son Lawrence, who became the Fourth Earl of Rosse.

When William Parsons, Third Earl of Rosse, died at Monkstown, County Dublin, in 1867, the "Leviathan" was still the largest telescope in the world. It was not to be equaled until 1919, when another 72-inch reflector was mounted in British Columbia, at the Dominion Astrophysical Observatory in Victoria. By that time the telescope at Birr Castle had been dismantled. By 1908 the protective walls had begun to crumble in the dampness and the whole structure became unsafe. That year the young Earl had his father's telescope taken down and sent the great mirror to London, to the Science Museum in South Kensington, where it is still exhibited.

Lord Rosse's 6-foot mirror was the last of the great metal mirrors. Later telescope objectives were made of glass, sur-

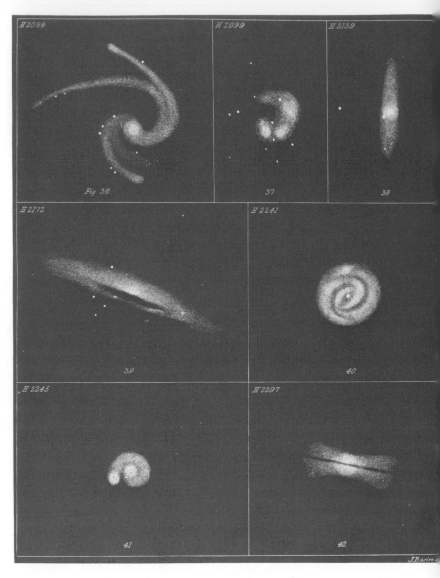

Sketches of nebulae, illustrating a paper delivered by Lord Rosse in 1850, when shown in negative are remarkably similar to photographs made nearly a century later with the 200-inch Hale telescope.

134

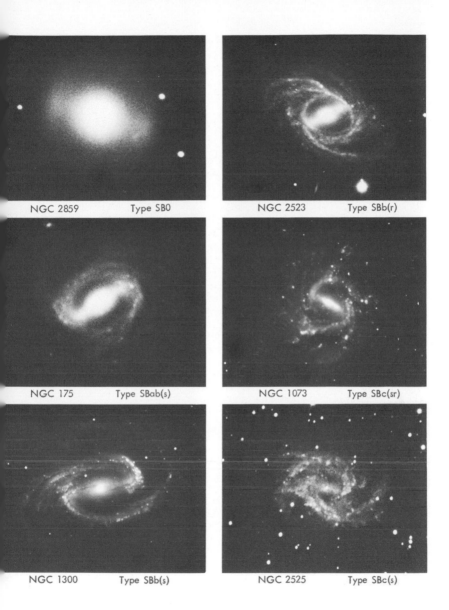

NGC 2859 Type SB0

NGC 2523 Type SBb(r)

NGC 175 Type SBab(s)

NGC 1073 Type SBc(sr)

NGC 1300 Type SBb(s)

NGC 2525 Type SBc(s)

135

faced with silver. The process, discovered in 1856 by a German physicist, Carl August von Steinheil, produced an almost perfect reflector. The comparatively low cost of glass, as compared to metal, made a big difference in the next century when the biggest reflectors were built.

The "Leviathan" of Parsonstown was still unsurpassed in 1865 when the French novelist Jules Verne mentioned it in his fantasy *From the Earth to the Moon*. Lord Rosse's telescope, Verne explained, magnified 6,400 times but was not powerful enough to observe the arrival on the moon of Verne's fictional rocket, manned by members of the American Gun Club. So, in Verne's tale, the rich Americans commissioned the Observatory of Cambridge, Massachusetts, to build a telescope of unheard-of dimensions. The fictional telescope, with a mirror sixteen feet (192 inches) in diameter, was built on a mountain top "in the territory of Missouri"—at a cost of $440,000.

It was only a fantasy, at the time. But eighty-three years later, on an American mountaintop, a telescope that surpassed Jules Verne's fantastic creation began to probe the sky. Its object glass was 200 inches in diameter, and it had cost more than six million dollars to build.

7

GEORGE ELLERY HALE'S VIEW FROM PALOMAR

More than a thousand people gathered on Palomar Mountain on June 3, 1948, for the dedication of the world's largest telescope. For twenty years astronomers had been waiting for the completion of the 200-inch reflector—a powerful eye that would make it possible for them to see eight times as much of the universe as they had been able to see before. Many of them had come to this California mountaintop—along with other scientists, government leaders, educators, and heads of wealthy foundations—to honor George Ellery Hale, the man who had made the telescope possible.

The crowd was hushed as Dr. Lee DuBridge, president of the California Institute of Technology in Pasadena, read a resolution from the Board of Trustees: ". . . that the 200-inch telescope of the Palomar Mountain Observatory shall hereafter be known as THE HALE TELESCOPE."

Applause thundered through the clear air and echoed off the neighboring peaks. As it faded Dr. DuBridge continued:

By this action the Board of Trustees seeks to recognize the great achievements of Dr. George Ellery Hale, who served as di-

George Ellery Hale (1868–1938).

rector of the Mount Wilson Observatory from 1904 to 1923, who served as a member of the Board of Trustees of the California Institute from 1907 to 1938, who originated the bold conception of the 200-inch telescope and whose brilliant leadership made possible its design and construction.

As other speakers paid their tribute, members of the audience who had worked with Dr. Hale wished that their former colleague might have lived to see his telescope in use. The astrophysicist and inventor had died in 1938 while the 20-ton mirror was being polished in the Cal Tech optical shop. Soon after his death the outbreak of World War II interrupted the work on his telescope. Ten more years went by before the huge instrument was mounted and ready to explore the sky.

In the twentieth-century astronomer's world there could be no more one-man telescopes. During the hundred years or more since William Herschel had built his first giants with his own hands, telescope making had grown far too complex and expensive for any one man to make the instruments for major observatories. But the ideas for these instruments originated in the minds of men like George Ellery Hale.

The Palomar giant was Hale's final triumph as a creator of telescopes but it was not his first. Before he turned to reflecting telescopes he had been responsible for the building of the 40-inch refractor at the Yerkes Observatory, still the largest lens telescope in the world. Then came the 60-inch reflector at Mount Wilson, California, and the 100-inch mirror that was the world's largest until the completion of the 200-inch reflector at Palomar.

The dedication of the Hale Telescope came almost exactly eighty years after George Ellery Hale was born, on June 29, 1868, just a year after Lord Rosse died. His parents, William Ellery Hale and Mary Scranton Browne Hale, lived in the heart of Chicago. When he was two years old his family moved from midtown LaSalle Street to a large new house in suburban Hyde Park. A year later George Hale's birthplace burned to the ground, along with every other house in the neighborhood, during the Chicago Fire of 1871.

Even as a child George Hale showed a scientist's curiosity. He collected rocks, fossils, and bugs; experimented with mixtures that smoked, bubbled, or exploded; built mechanical gadgets; and begged his parents for a laboratory. His mother cleared out an upstairs room for him and wrote to his grandmother, "Georgie spends all the time he can get in his shop . . . and we hope he will learn a good deal from his tinkering." George's younger brother Will and his sister Martha were his willing assistants.

George's father encouraged his son's interests and gave him whatever equipment he needed, whenever George could convince him that it was for a worthwhile purpose. William Hale could afford to be generous. Most of the new skyscrapers rising out of the ruins of the Chicago Fire were furnished with hydraulic elevators made by the Hale Construction Company. Orders poured in from other cities, then from other countries. The prosperous Hales were about to become rich.

George Hale's interest in the stars began so early that he could never remember, later, exactly when or how it started. His mother showed him some constellations before he was old enough to go to school. He could remember his delight

The 200-inch Palomar telescope became a monument to Hale.

in Jules Verne's tale, *From the Earth to the Moon*, when an uncle read it to him. As a schoolboy his interests were outside the classroom—exploring Chicago with the Owl Bicycle Club, reading *The Boy Engineers*, working in his "shop," putting on magic shows with his friend and classmate, Burton Holmes. The two boys talked about a stage career as "The Boy Magicians."

When Hale was thirteen or fourteen he first tried to make a telescope. The idea may have come to him while reading *Cassell's Book of Sports and Pastimes*, a Christmas present from his mother in 1881. The telescope didn't work very well, but because of it he met a professional astronomer who introduced him to his future.

A neighbor of the Hales in Hyde Park was Sherburne Wesley Burnham, an astronomer who had once worked at the Lick Observatory in California. Now he worked as a court reporter in the daytime and devoted his nights to star watching with a telescope set up in a backyard shed. Young George Hale took his unsuccessful telescope to Burnham and asked his advice. It was the beginning of a friendship that led George straight to his life's work.

Burnham told George about a secondhand telescope he had seen. It had an excellent 4-inch lens—one of the best made by the well-known American lens maker and astronomer Alvan Clark. It was for sale at a bargain price. George asked his father for the money and was refused—at first. Day after day, whenever he had the chance, George explained to his father why he wanted the telescope so desperately before the sixth of December. On that date in 1882 Venus would cross the face of the sun, a rare celestial event to be watched by astronomers all over the world. George wanted to be one of those astronomers. William Hale said nothing.

Early in December William Hale came home one day with a long wooden box containing the precious telescope. On the evening of the sixth, while his younger brother and sister watched, George set it up before an open window in his mother's bedroom. Martha and Will shivered in the winter air while he timed the transit of Venus as it moved across the sun, from one edge to the other. From that night on, he kept an astronomer's notebook, listing his observations with details of time and weather.

The following spring George began experimenting with a camera attached to his telescope. Soon the walls of his workshop were decorated with pictures of the craters of the moon, a partial eclipse of the sun, and various planets. By this time he had built himself a real shop in a backyard shed, equipped with a lathe run by a steam engine he had made from a secondhand boiler, an old stove, and some pipe.

One day George went with his friend Burnham to the Dearborn Observatory in Chicago and met the white-bearded director, George Washington Hough. The two older men gave the young astronomer a tour of the observatory and showed him the 18½-inch refractor, the largest telescope George had ever seen. A few minutes later Hough offered George a part-time job running the engine that turned the observatory dome and making routine observations to keep the clocks accurate for the Chicago Board of Trade. George accepted enthusiastically. So, while still in high school, he found himself working with a distinguished astronomer in a major observatory.

Before his graduation from high school in 1886 George Ellery Hale knew that he wanted to devote his life to science. Before the year was over he had begun a study of the sun that was to occupy the rest of his life. That same year he finished high school, entered college, traveled to Europe with his family, proposed to the girl he intended to marry, and launched a scientific research project.

Early in 1886, when George was only seventeen, he built a spectroscope, following the instructions given in his treasured copy of *Cassell's Book of Sports and Pastimes*. Using a prism from an old candelabrum, some cardboard tubes, a pair of old spectacle lenses, and a brass plate with a slit cut into it, he made an instrument that split the light of a candle flame into a vividly colored rainbow. He was so delighted with his observations that he decided to build a larger instrument, also described in *Cassell's*, using a hollow prism filled with carbon disulfide. The family complained about the smell of burning sulfur, but George didn't seem to notice the odor. With his new spectroscope he examined light from the salted wick of a spirit lamp and saw the bright yellow sodium line, just as *Cassell's* predicted.

The next day he mounted a mirror in his window to reflect sunlight into his spectroscope. As the rainbow colors spread out before him he could see the dark lines of the sun's spectrum, as Joseph Fraunhofer had seen them more than seventy years earlier. "I was," Hale remembered, "completely carried off my feet. From that moment my fate was sealed."

I cannot think without excitement [Hale wrote later] of my first faint perception of the possibilities of the spectroscope and my first glimpse of the pathway then suggested for me. No other research can surpass in interest and importance that of interpreting the mysteries concealed in these lines. Their positions and intensities, and the extraordinary change they may undergo as the result of variations in the physical and chemical state of the vapors that produce them, afford the chief clue to the nature and evolution of the sun and stars, and to the constitution of matter itself.

With his homemade spectroscope seventeen-year-old George Hale began to measure the lines in the sun's spectrum, intending to find out for himself what the sun is made of. He read everything he could find on the subject. In the seventy years since Fraunhofer's discovery of the magic lines, many scientists had used them to unlock mysteries of the universe. Even before Kirchhoff announced the three laws that became the basis for all spectroscopy, Sir William Huggins in England and Angelo Secchi in Italy were studying Fraunhofer lines in the spectra of stars.

Hale read books by and about these men. He was particularly fascinated by the work of Norman Lockyer, a contemporary English astronomer who had used Fraunhofer lines to study the sun and had discovered an element unknown on earth. He called it *helium*, after *helios*, the Greek word for sun. More than twenty years later helium was found in the earth's atmosphere, but when George Hale was seventeen, helium on earth was unknown. What could be more exciting than to discover a new, unknown element? George Hale considered Lockyer's discovery a challenge. He devoured Lockyer's *Solar Physics* and *Studies in Spectrum Analysis*.

That summer, while the Hales were traveling in Europe

with George's school friend Burton Holmes and his family, George bought the instrument that made his reputation as a serious scientist before he was twenty-one. In London the two boys went to a shop to buy a few magic tricks for their shows at home, but George only watched while Burton made his selections and paid for them. He saved his money until they went to Browning's, an optical shop famous for its scientific instruments.

Burton was shocked at his friend's extravagance. "He squandered forty pounds," Burton said, "on funny-looking things which meant nothing to me." One of these was a spectroscope, George's treasured possession for many years, even after he became director of an observatory with much finer instruments at his command.

In the fall of 1886 George Hale entered the Massachusetts Institute of Technology. On his way to Boston he stopped in New York to see Evelina Conklin, a girl he had met four or five years earlier in Madison, Connecticut, where his family and the Conklins often spent their summers. George had decided—as definitely and surely as he had decided to follow a career in science—that he was going to marry Evelina. It was only two months after his eighteenth birthday, and he knew that they were too young to be married yet, but he had made up his mind to marry Evelina just as soon as he received his degree from M.I.T. Since he was so sure about it, he thought he might as well tell her.

He proposed and she accepted. Considering himself engaged, George wrote to his parents to tell them the news, then went on to Boston, feeling very satisfied that another major decision had been settled. A few days later he was stunned to receive anxious letters from his father and Evelina's, telling him he had been "'overhasty." He and Evelina were "much too young," the letters reminded him; the engagement was "premature." George was upset by the tone of the letters, but they didn't change anything. He and Evelina had planned to wait four years anyway.

During those four years George endured M.I.T. without really liking it, regarding his classes as interruptions of the work he really wanted to do. In the summers he hurried home to his own laboratory, a small red brick building his father had built for him on the new family estate in Kenwood, an elegant Chicago suburb. George was outfitting it as a spectroscopic observatory and he called it the Kenwood Physical Laboratory.

In the middle of his sophomore year George wrote to Edward Pickering of the Harvard Observatory in Cambridge, asking for a job as a volunteer helper on Saturdays. Pickering invited him to come for an interview, and the job was his. After that, George lived for Saturdays, when he traveled to Cambridge by horsecar to work among the astronomers at Harvard. At first he merely took care of the instruments and did some routine photography. Later he was allowed to attach his spectroscope to the 15-inch refractor to continue his analysis of the sun's spectrum.

In the summer of 1888, just after his twentieth birthday, George Hale made a discovery that gained him the respect of the scientists he most admired. Working in his own Kenwood laboratory, he identified carbon in the sun's spectrum. Other scientists had debated the presence of carbon, but young George Hale was the first to offer photographic proof that it was there.

The following summer, after some unsuccessful attempts

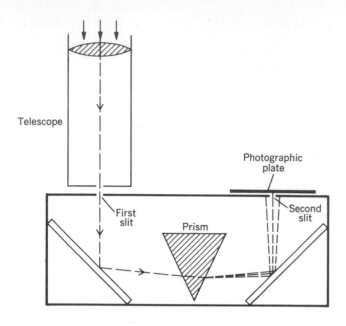

Hale's Spectroheliograph

to photograph the sun, George conceived, diagramed, and tried to build a device he called a *spectroheliograph*. He wanted to photograph the solar prominences—those towering flames or clouds of hot gas that appear at the edge of the sun's disc. Photographs of these prominences had been made during eclipses of the sun, but George wanted to photograph them without waiting for an eclipse, without traveling to some far-off place where an eclipse might be visible. Ordinary photographic equipment could not capture the sun's image without the film becoming fogged by the powerful glare. Young Hale's device would make it possible to find out what solar prominences are made of by photographing the sun in the light of one element at a time.

As he described it:

148

The principle of this instrument is very simple. Its object is to build up on a photographic plate a picture of the solar flames, by recording side by side images of the bright spectral lines which characterize the luminous gases. In the first place, an image of the sun is formed by a telescope on the slit of the spectroscope. The light of the sun, after transmission through the spectroscope, is spread out into a long band of color, crossed by lines representing the various elements. At points where the slit of the spectroscope happens to intersect a gaseous prominence, the bright lines of hydrogen may be seen extending from the base of the prominence to its outer boundary. If a series of such lines, corresponding to different postitions of the slit on the image of the prominence, were registered side by side on a photographic plate, it is obvious that they would give a representation of the form of the prominence itself.

He explained how this could be accomplished by using another slit behind a lens on the other side of the prism of the spectroscope to capture light of one color only. The single color passes through the slit and registers on the photographic plate. Since this particular wavelength could come from only one element on the sun, the resulting photograph would be a "picture" of that element. The slit could be adjusted to admit other wavelengths, one at a time, to build up a picture of other elements present.

The device didn't work too well with George's small telescope at home. When he returned to school in the fall, he took his spectroheliograph with him, impatient to try it out with the superior instruments at the Harvard Observatory. Before long the Harvard astronomers were swarming around Hale and his device, fascinated by the experiments of an inventor who wasn't even a Harvard man. Meanwhile, George Hale's schoolwork at M.I.T. was going downhill, except for the physics course in which he was writing a thesis on "The Photography of Solar Prominences."

By the end of his senior year, in May 1890, some of his grades were barely passing, but he was nevertheless recommended for a bachelor's degree in physics. Meanwhile, at Harvard he had improved his spectroheliograph and had produced some crude but promising photographs of solar prominences. The word was getting around to other observatories that George Ellery Hale was a young man to watch.

On June 3, two days after his graduation, George Hale and Evelina Conklin were married at her parents' house in Brooklyn. Immediately afterward the couple set out on a coast-to-coast wedding trip, from New York to California, by way of Niagara Falls, Chicago, Yosemite National Park, and the Garden of the Gods. For George the focal point of the whole trip was the Lick Observatory at Mount Hamilton, California.

George and his bride climbed the mountain in a horse-drawn stagecoach, rattling and bouncing along steeply twisting roads through scenery that seemed wild and rugged to the New York girl. Evelina Hale never forgot that strange night they spent on the mountain. For hours she listened in silence while her young husband talked about astrophysics with his fellow scientists. The observatory director, Edward S. Holden, offered George a job at Lick, where he could use his spectroheliograph with the observatory's 36-inch refractor, then the largest in the world. George was so tempted by the offer that Evelina was afraid she might have to spend the rest of her life on this wild and isolated mountain, but she said nothing. George didn't make up his mind right away. He had received other offers—and he hadn't yet decided where to work for his Ph.D.

Back in Chicago, George asked his father's advice and was persuaded to refuse Holden's offer—and all others. With the help of his wealthy father, George could build his own observatory, as an addition to the Kenwood Physical Laboratory. William Hale offered to provide a 12-inch telescope, made to order, with a mounting designed to hold the spectroheliograph. Without leaving home George could continue his study of the sun. For a while he hesitated, still tempted by the opportunity to work at Lick, but eventually his father won.

Within a year George Ellery Hale was a recognized authority on the sun, contributing scientific papers to learned journals in the United States and abroad. Before his twenty-second birthday the Kenwood Physical Observatory had become a "legally organized corporation" under Illinois state law and its young director had been elected a fellow of the Royal Astronomical Society of Great Britain. Later that summer, when he and Evelina were traveling in Europe, George Hale was received by distinguished astronomers and physicists as a fellow scientist.

A year later, in July 1892, George Hale was appointed Associate Professor of Astral Physics and Director of the Observatory for the new University of Chicago. The university had no observatory of its own, but Kenwood was made available to it, along with the young professor. William Hale, who had poured thousands of dollars into his son's observatory, agreed to give the university "the movable apparatus and instruments at the Kenwood Observatory . . . on condition that within one year from that time, the

University shall secure good subscriptions to an Astronomical fund, to be expended for an observatory, of not less than two hundred and fifty thousand dollars."

To raise that much money in a year required a special kind of talent. The president of the University of Chicago, William Rainey Harper, kept an eye on his new associate professor whose father had influential friends all over the world. On an October morning in 1892 George Ellery Hale found himself in the office of Chicago millionaire Charles Tyson Yerkes, with the president of the University of Chicago at his elbow. His assignment: to persuade the crotchety millionaire to put up the money to build a telescope for the university.

When the two men left Yerkes's office they had a check for $20,000, enough to buy two superb 40-inch discs of crown and flint glass, already waiting in the workshop of Alvan Clark, the great American lens maker. They would have to collect at least twenty times that amount of money if they were to have the discs ground into a lens, mounted in a telescope, and housed in an observatory. At least they had begun.

George Ellery Hale didn't enjoy fund raising, but he did enjoy planning the observatory. It would be like no other observatory on earth—with spectroscopic instruments, a photographic darkroom, and all the facilities necessary to make it a physical laboratory as well as an observatory. He described it in detail to dozens of wealthy men—all of whom turned him down. Returning to Yerkes, he persuaded the trolley-car magnate to pay for mounting the telescope. Before he was through, Yerkes had written enough checks to build the whole observatory.

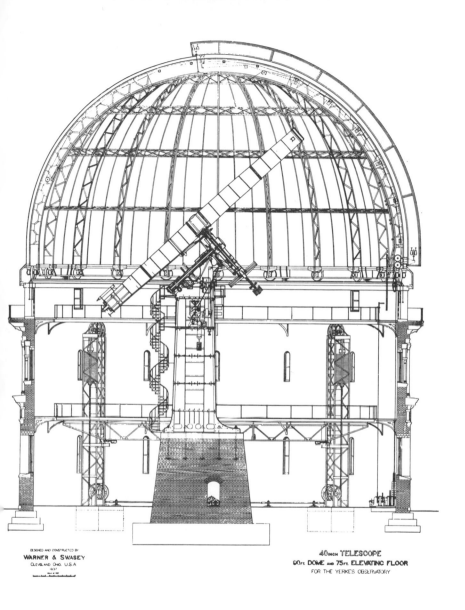

40 INCH TELESCOPE
90 ft. DOME AND 75 ft. ELEVATING FLOOR
FOR THE YERKES OBSERVATORY

Charles Yerkes, a Chicago millionaire, financed the observatory Hale
had dreamed of, designed to house the world's largest refractor.

153

The University of Chicago had to wait much longer than one year for its own observatory, but it was worth waiting for. On October 21, 1897, the Yerkes Observatory was dedicated at Williams Bay, Wisconsin. It was the first of its kind—a complete astrophysical laboratory equipped with the largest refracting telescope in the world, 40 inches in diameter. George Ellery Hale, at twenty-nine, became its first director.

Astronomers flocked to Yerkes from other states, then from England, Germany, Russia, and as far away as India to work without pay in the interest of science. While they compared notes on their research about the stars, the director pursued his study of our own star, the sun. With his spectroheliograph attached to the 40-inch refractor he was able to observe details he had never been able to see at Kenwood. As he photographed the bright solar flames, carefully measuring the motion and velocity of the whirling hot gases, he began to understand more about the sun's stormy atmosphere.

Within five years at Yerkes, George Hale was looking for new frontiers to conquer. If he were going to carry his research further, he needed a different kind of telescope. He had to gather more light, but a lens larger than his 40-inch refractor was impractical. Even if a larger one could be made and mounted—no small challenge—it would *not* necessarily gather more light. Such a lens would be so thick that it would absorb more light than it allowed to pass through. With the 40-inch Yerkes refractor, telescope making had reached a point where any increase in diameter would mean a decrease in light. George Hale began to think of installing a large reflector at Yerkes.

The observatory already owned a 60-inch glass disc, cast in France at the expense of William Hale, but it was still resting in a basement, waiting for some miracle to provide the hundreds of thousands of dollars necessary to transform it into a reflecting telescope and house it in an appropriate dome. In 1902 George Hale thought such a miracle might be coming his way. He read that the wealthy Andrew Carnegie had founded an institution "to encourage investigation, research, and discovery in the broadest and most liberal manner, and the application of knowledge to the improvement of mankind." Carnegie's initial gift to the institution was ten million dollars.

With Carnegie's help, Hale built his 60-inch telescope, but by the time it became a reality in 1908, he was already at work on an even larger one. A 100-inch mirror was being polished in the optical shop of a brand-new solar observatory on Mount Wilson, near Pasadena, California. George Ellery Hale had founded a second great observatory and had become its director.

Even before the 60-inch reflector was ready to be used, Hale and his spectroheliograph had uncovered a secret of the sun that had puzzled astronomers for three hundred years. What are sunspots? Hale discovered that they are gigantic magnetic fields produced by huge whirling tornadoes of hydrogen. The world's scientists cheered him. The president of the Carnegie Institution, physicist Robert S. Woodward, wrote: "This is surely the greatest advance that has been made since Galileo's discovery of those blemishes on the sun." *The New York Times* called Hale a "Priest of the Sun," responsible for "a whole new solar philosophy."

It was the happiest and most productive time of Hale's

life. In 1908 he was just forty years old, still happily married to Evelina and the father of twelve-year-old Margaret and eight-year-old William. His family was settled in a flower-covered house in Pasadena, feeling more at home than they had ever felt in wintry Williams Bay. In spite of his busy schedule at Mount Wilson, George Hale found time to enjoy his family and friends—and to serve as trustee for a small technical school in Pasadena, Throop Institute.

Hale was confident that Throop could become a first-rate scientific institute, comparable to the best in Germany and Sweden. He envisioned a school that would train imaginative research scientists, not mere technicians. His enthusiasm and hard work attracted world-famous scientists to the lecture halls of Throop. Many of them stayed to become part of the faculty. Eventually, in 1920, Throop Institute became the California Institute of Technology, destined to educate more Nobel Prize winners than any other school in the world.

Meanwhile, on Mount Wilson, the 100-inch telescope was finally mounted, after ten years of false starts, financial disappointments, and technical difficulties. In his diary Hale made a brief note:

Friday, November 2, 1917—With Alfred Noyes to Mountain. First Observations with 100"—Jupiter, Moon, Saturn.
November 3, 1917—To Pasadena.

Hale's companion wrote about that night in greater detail. Alfred Noyes, the English poet known to every high school student as author of "The Highwayman," later published *Watchers of the Sky*, an epic poem about the astronomers on Mount Wilson.

After its completion in 1917, the 100-inch Hooker reflecting telescope at Mount Wilson became the astronomers' mecca.

The mountain became the astronomers' mecca. Physicists, mathematicians, and chemists followed. Albert Einstein, James Jeans, Arthur Eddington, Harlow Shapley, Edwin Hubble, Albert Michelson, and Edward Morley were only a few of the visitors who made fundamental discoveries about the universe while working at Mount Wilson. But for every question that was answered by the men who used the 100-inch telescope, a hundred more arose, demanding to be investigated. If these questions, too, were to be answered, astronomers had to gather more light. The world's largest telescope was not large enough.

George Ellery Hale spent twenty satisfying years at

Mount Wilson, until ill health forced him to retire in 1923. After 1910 he had suffered several severe physical break-downs and his doctors ordered him to "slow down." They were talking to a dynamo who didn't know how to slow down. In 1923 he was told firmly that he was not to climb the mountain. He was to limit his working hours at home and was to drop as many outside responsibilities as possible. But nobody could forbid George Hale to think and plan. In an armchair in his Pasadena library he began to dream of a bigger telescope that would gather more light.

In the early years at Mount Wilson he had written: "It is impossible to predict the dimensions that reflecting tele-scopes will ultimately attain." Since writing those words, he had seen what could be done with a 100-inch reflector. How much more could be learned about the universe with a tele-scope two or three times that size! When he was asked to write an article for *Harper's* magazine in 1928, he set down some of his ideas on "The Possibilities of Large Tele-scopes."

The article was scheduled for the April issue of *Harper's*. Hale sent an advance proof to Dr. Wickliffe Rose of the Rockefeller Foundation, suggesting that some day the foun-dation might be interested in sponsoring a large telescope, perhaps 200 or 300 inches in diameter. Rose's prompt reply surprised him a few days later. The foundation was "inter-ested" and invited Dr. Hale to come to New York to dis-cuss the idea.

Within two months the Rockefeller Foundation had voted to give the largest telescope in the world to the Cali-fornia Institute of Technology and had provided six million dollars for the purpose. George Ellery Hale was named chairman of Cal Tech's Observatory Council and was already calling in experts to plan and design a 200-inch reflecting telescope.

On his sixtieth birthday in June 1928 he wrote wistfully, "I wish I were thirty years younger and able to jump into the task as I did at Mount Wilson." He was trying to follow his doctor's advice, but the telescope was too important to him. He was never content to be a spectator while others did the work.

With six million dollars at its disposal, the Cal Tech Observatory Council was confident that a 200-inch reflecting telescope could be built, in spite of the problems involved in making and mounting its large mirror. The first problem was to select the right material. It would be glass, but what kind of glass?

Ordinary glass wouldn't do because it is elastic, expanding with heat and contracting with cold. A telescope mirror, if it is to be dependable, must be nearly immune to temperature changes. Some of the finest optical glass is fused quartz, pure silica crystals (silicon dioxide) melted at high temperatures into a homogeneous mass. When it cools, it becomes a clear tough glass that expands very little when heated. Fused quartz was expensive, but the Observatory Council wanted the best possible mirror for the new telescope. They set aside part of the budget for a fused quartz mirror.

After three years of unsuccessful experiments with test mirrors, Cal Tech optical experts reported that a very large quartz mirror might crack while cooling. Perhaps another material would be better. The Corning glass works in New York state had developed a strong, heat-resistant glass called *pyrex.* Maybe this would be the ideal material for the new mirror.

A pyrex mirror would be cheaper than quartz but much heavier. A 200-inch disc would weigh about forty-two tons and would be all but impossible to mount. On the other hand, it would provide a superb reflecting surface. Hale felt that the advantages of pyrex outweighed the disadvantages. If a successful 200-inch mirror could be made, some way would be found to mount it.

Then the designers hit upon an idea for making a 200-inch pyrex disc that would weigh no more than half as much as they had calculated at first. Since the disc was being made for a mirror, not a lens, it need not be *solid* pyrex. The reflecting surface was the most important part. The rest of the disc could be full of holes—a honeycomb of pyrex behind a relatively thin, solid disc to be ground to the proper shape, polished, and coated with aluminum. The disc could be made by pouring molten pyrex into a mold equipped with metal cores arranged so as to leave a network of holes in the glass. The Observatory Council agreed to have the disc for the mirror made at Corning.

In March 1934, six years after the planning began, the disc had not yet been poured, but George Hale was full of hope. Early that month he went to Mount Palomar, south of Pasadena, to look at a possible site for the world's largest telescope. He found Palomar "ideal." The papers for obtaining the site were signed.

Two weeks later the big pyrex mirror was poured in Corning, New York. Hale wanted to be there but his doctor wouldn't allow it. The next day he learned that he had missed a disaster. During the pouring several metal cores in-

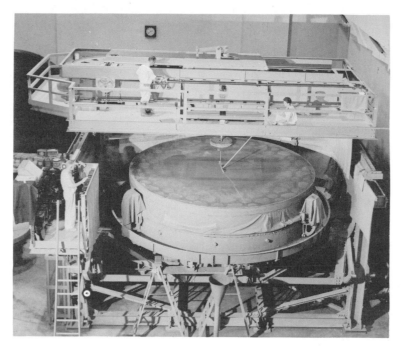

Ready and in place for polishing, the 200-inch mirror of the Hale telescope was carefully protected from dust in the optical shop.

side the mold had come loose and had floated around in the molten glass. A second pouring, scheduled for December, was successful. Then began a long, slow, carefully controlled cooling process called *annealing*. This was Corning's secret for making pyrex tough and heatproof.

Two years later the giant pyrex disc began the long journey from New York to California, along a special route worked out to avoid narrow roads, bridges, and tunnels. The disc traveled on a flat-bed trailer, specially built to fit it and shockproofed as carefully as if the cargo had been explosives. The precious disc arrived safely at Pasadena in April

161

GIANT PATH TO PRIME FOCUS. f 3.3
CASSEGRAIN = f 16
COUDE = f 30

APPROXIMATE SCALE

R. W. PORTER. '38

THE TWO HUNDRED INCH TELESCOPE~

Designs for Hale's giant were drawn by an amateur astronomer and artist, R. W. Porter. The original drawings now hang in the Robinson Astrophysics Laboratory at California Institute of Technology.

1936 and was delivered to a new optical shop built for it on the Cal Tech campus. Rough grinding was begun.

By 1938 a dome was being built on Palomar Mountain—a dome the size of the Pantheon in Rome—to house the 200-inch giant. The great pyrex disc had been ground and was ready to be polished. Soon the huge metal horseshoe mounting, weighing more than a hundred and fifty tons, would be on its way to California by ship. The man who made the telescope possible longed to go to Palomar to see the work in progress. But George Ellery Hale, disabled by arteriosclerosis, was being cared for at a sanitarium in Pasadena.

When he died, on February 21, 1938, an editorial in *The New York Times* suggested that "some fitting monument should be erected in his memory." The monument was already being built on Mount Palomar. Ten years later it was officially named "The Hale Telescope."

8

BERNHARD SCHMIDT'S
SKY CAMERA

On Palomar Mountain, about a quarter of a mile east of the largest telescope in the world, there is a smaller dome which houses the 200-inch giant's most valuable assistant, a remarkable telescope-camera affectionately called "The Big Schmidt." It is both a reflector and a refractor. This ingenious combination of mirror and lens has given astronomers a comprehensive view of the universe that was impossible before the Big Schmidt was built.

The Hale telescope looks billions of miles into space, but it gives a narrow view of those remote regions, showing only a tiny area at a time. For an overall picture of the sky—all that can be seen from Palomar Mountain with the 200-inch telescope—astronomers would have to piece together millions of individual photographs. How much more efficiently an overall view can be obtained with a telescope that sees far and wide at the same time! That is what the 48-inch Schmidt telescope does.

The Big Schmidt was installed at Palomar in the autumn of 1948. In July 1949 it was used by a team of astronomers to begin a systematic photographic survey of the sky. In 1956 a

Bernhard Schmidt (1879–1935).

sky atlas consisting of 1,758 celestial photographs was completed. But the story of the Big Schmidt began a long way from Palomar Mountain, at least half a century before the telescope-camera began its first major assignment. As early as 1903 in Germany, the man who invented it, Bernhard Schmidt, was at work on the idea.

The taciturn young man with one arm was a familiar figure among the regular patrons of Bretschneider's Lindengarten restaurant in Mittweida, Germany. He didn't talk to the other customers very much but he always greeted Frau Bretschneider when he came in—sometimes several times in a single evening. By 1903 the Lindengarten regulars were no longer surprised when he came in the front door, nodded briefly to the proprietress, marched directly to the back door, and went out again. Nor were they surprised if an hour or two later he marched back in the opposite direction.

By this time they knew that Bernhard Schmidt was a rather eccentric young lens grinder who liked to look at the stars. His workshop was set up in an abandoned bowling alley behind the Lindengarten and his outdoor observatory was in an open lot across the street from the front door of the tavern. When going from one to the other, he could save a lot of time if he took a short cut through the Lindengarten.

When he walked through on winter nights, with a woolen muffler around his neck and the empty right sleeve of his coat pinned up to keep out the wind, he sometimes stopped at the bar to have a glass of brandy. "To raise my potential energy," he told Frau Bretschneider. After warming his left hand at the big Nuremberg stove he would go out into the freezing air to spend the rest of the night with his telescope.

Schmidt's outdoor observatory was in an open lot in Mittweida.

From time to time he would come back inside for a while, to warm up with another glass of brandy and toast his frozen fingers.

Nobody was quite sure what Bernhard Schmidt was trying to do in his observatory. He was certainly a very earnest young man, no more than twenty-five years old—too absorbed in his work to join in any of the social activities of the young people of Mittweida. Somebody said he had rigged up a camera to take pictures of the moon and stars through his telescope. If anybody asked him about his work he seemed unwilling to talk about it very much—as he seemed unwilling to talk about himself.

Once, in a particularly talkative mood, he told the proprietress of the Lindengarten that he had to move to a new

167

boardinghouse because his landlady had thrown him out. She had objected to his use of a finely finished chest of drawers as a work table for polishing his lenses. But he never talked about where he came from or why, or how he had lost his arm.

Because Schmidt didn't volunteer any information, the townspeople hesitated to ask him about himself—and so they speculated. Some wondered if his name were really Schmidt. Such a common German name—like Smith in English! Just the kind of name a man might give if he didn't want to give his real one. There was a rumor that this Bernhard Schmidt wasn't even a native German. He spoke German fluently enough, with no foreign accent, but those with sharp ears detected something about his speech—an inflection or tone—that sounded slightly Baltic. Was he Polish? Or perhaps Scandinavian? It was hard to tell about his appearance. His light brown hair, blue eyes, and not-very-large frame might have been Danish, or Polish, or even German, after all.

If the townspeople had asked directly, Schmidt might have told them enough to clear up the mystery. He was Estonian, born on the island of Naissaar in the Gulf of Finland on March 30, 1879. His name was, truly and legally, Bernhard Voldemar Schmidt. His family was not German, but an ancestor named Matts had taken the name Schmidt at a time when Germans were the ruling class in Estonia. Many Estonians, especially businessmen and professionals, found that a German name could be the key to success. So Bernhard grew up with the name Schmidt and he spoke German all his life.

As far back as he could remember, Bernhard Schmidt had

been interested in the stars, and a lot of other things besides. When he was about twelve years old he experimented with making gunpowder. His parents encouraged most of his interests, but his mother was uneasy about the gunpowder and warned him, as mothers do, please to be careful. One Sunday when the rest of the family was at church, Bernhard tried to make a rocket by stuffing an iron pipe with gunpowder. What he made was a powerful bomb. When he lit the fuse the bomb exploded—and took off his right arm.

After that he dabbled with other apparatus, including lenses and cameras. Later in his life some of Schmidt's colleagues liked to tell a story about a telescope lens that he made, when he was a young boy, from the bottom of an old broken bottle he found on the beach at Naissaar. According to the story, the boy ground his lens with sand from the beach, rubbing the broken glass in a saucer filled with sand until he had shaped a lens. Like other stories about other telescope makers, this one may or may not be true, but Bernhard Schmidt's later accomplishments make it believable.

His brother described him as a boy "of very, very few words. . . . Among other children he was very shy, often lost in thought, but always busy with something interesting."

In 1895, when Bernhard was sixteen, he became a telegraph operator for the Estonian Coast Guard station at Reval (now Tallin), on the mainland coast near his island birthplace. He went on to a variety of other jobs: as a retoucher for a photographer for a while, then in 1898 as an employee of the Volta company, a manufacturer of electrical instruments. All this time he continued to spend his off-duty hours experimenting with lenses and telescopes—and watching the stars whenever he could. The nights were too short in summer, in that northern latitude, for much concentrated star gazing. But in winter, when darkness fell in mid-afternoon and lingered until after his workday started, Bernhard spent long hours looking at the sky.

By the time he was nineteen, Bernhard Schmidt's name was becoming familiar to amateur astronomers who read a magazine called *Astronomische Rundschau* ("Astronomy Roundup"). He wrote frequent letters to the magazine, and after a while his name was mentioned often in its columns as an observer of various happenings in the sky—including the appearance of a *nova*.

Like Tycho Brahe in 1572 and Kepler in 1604, Bernhard Schmidt saw a bright star appear in the sky where no star had been visible before. Early astronomers who witnessed such rare celestial events thought they were seeing the births of new stars, so they called them *novae*, the Latin word for *new*. In Schmidt's time these stars were still unexplained, but astronomers had learned that they were not really new. Each nova had been there all the time, too faint to be seen until some violent explosion made it suddenly brighter for a while. Gradually it faded back to its original dimness. The ultra-bright apparitions seen by Tycho and Kepler were classified as *supernovae*. In 1901 Bernhard Schmidt was listed in *Astronomische Rundschau* as one of the discoverers of the nova in the constellation Perseus.

At about this time Bernhard Schmidt decided to do something about his education. He had dropped out of school very early and had taught himself lens grinding, but he realized that he needed more formal education. He had gone to Sweden in 1900 to attend the Chalmers Institute of Technology at Göteborg, but he left before the first term ended. Then in 1901 he entered an engineering school at Mittweida. At first he intended to stay "just a few terms," but he settled down so comfortably in Mittweida with his bowling-alley workshop and nearby observatory that he stayed for twenty-five years. During those years he became an expert on lenses, mirrors, cameras, and telescopes.

Astronomers of the early 1900's were still debating the relative advantages of refracting and reflecting telescopes. The sharp bright image produced by a good refractor such as Fraunhofer's was unbeatable. But the large reflectors, such as Herschel's and Lord Rosse's, probed more distant parts of the sky. A few experimenters had discovered a way to make the most of the light gathered by either type of telescope. A photographic plate, they discovered, could detect distant points of light that were invisible to the human eye, even at the eyepiece of the largest reflector.

Sky photography had its tentative beginnings more than sixty years before Bernhard Schmidt came to Mittweida. On March 23, 1840, a New York University professor and amateur photographer, John William Draper, made a daguerreotype of the moon. It wasn't a large picture. The image of the moon was only about an inch across, and the mountains and craters seen by Galileo through his spyglass were not visible in the picture. But it was an important experiment—the first genuine astronomical photograph.

The daguerreotype process was brand-new. Just a year before Draper's experiment, in 1839, the French government had bought the rights to the process from its inventor, Louis Jacques Daguerre. This French physicist, who was also a scene painter for the opera, had discovered that a metal or glass plate, coated with a thin film of silver iodide and exposed to a subject, could be developed by exposing it to mercury vapor. Daguerre's method was the answer to a question that had baffled experimenters since the Italian Giambattista della Porta, in Galileo's time, invented the pinhole camera: How could the image formed behind the camera's aperture be captured? Now, with the introduction of Daguerre's process, a new science was born. *Photography* was the name given to it by Sir John Herschel, astronomer-son of the great telescope maker, Sir William Herschel. It was Sir John who introduced the "hypo" solution (sodium hyposulfite) that fixed an image, preventing its fading from a Daguerre plate.

Ten years after Draper took his picture of the moon, the daguerreotype process had been improved and simplified. In 1850 another American, Harvard astronomer George P. Bond, made a photograph of the moon through a 15-inch refracting telescope. The picture, showing the moon's rough surface, was shown in London at the International Exhibition of 1851 and attracted thousands of curious viewers.

By the time Schmidt began his experiments with sky photography, Daguerre's rather clumsy process had led the way to faster and more efficient ones, but astronomers were still waiting for a really successful combination of camera and telescope. That was what Bernhard Schmidt intended to produce. His determination led eventually to the invention of the Schmidt telescope, or Schmidt camera—a telescope that was a camera.

In his Mittweida workshop Schmidt ground and polished lenses and mirrors that became better and better as he improved his technique. A polishing machine might have speeded up his production and provided an occasional rest for his overworked left arm, but he didn't approve of mechanical polishing. A machine could not *feel*, as his hand could, the heat generated by too much rubbing—treacherous heat that created flaws in a mirror.

"The machine makes mistakes," he said. "If the hand encounters friction, you have to stop work at once until the temperature is evened out. But your machine can't detect this; it polishes on mindlessly, warming up the place of the friction, and your defect gets bigger and bigger."

So Bernhard Schmidt insisted on polishing his mirrors by hand. With his one arm he produced mirrors of such remarkable quality that his fame spread among amateur astronomers, if not yet among professionals. An article in one of the astronomy magazines of 1903 praised his methods:

Mr. Schmidt has recently tried to remove trial and error from the process of grinding. . . . His method is almost mathematical in its reliability. . . . The artist Bernhard Schmidt has certainly achieved a tour de force, for he gave one mirror the remarkable focal ratio of f/5. He has earned the highest praise if he can give such perfection to so short a reflector.

It was a remarkable accomplishment. The "f" number of a lens or mirror represents the focal length divided by the diameter. If Schmidt's mirror were four inches across, with a focal ratio of f/5, it would require a tube only twenty inches long. Earlier telescope makers would have housed a four-inch mirror in a tube nearly twice as long.

But with all the perfection of his mirrors, Schmidt was not able to take the kind of sky photographs he wanted to take. If only he had access to a large reflecting telescope, he felt he could capture the light from distant stars and nebulae never seen by the human eye, but he certainly could not hope to own such a telescope. The mounting for the kind of telescope he had in mind would be expensive even for a rich man—and Bernhard Schmidt was not rich. Perhaps he could arrange to use a telescope at one of the large observatories.

By 1904, when he was twenty-five, Schmidt felt ready to seek attention from professional astronomers. On May 29 of that year he wrote a letter to the Astrophysical Observatory in Potsdam.

"Permit me to ask," he began, "whether you are interested in reflecting telescopes. I would gladly provide a large mirror for the observatory at my own cost, so that I could find out what a large mirror could do photographically after it is mounted."

In the letter he enclosed some pictures—one of the moon and several of star trails—and described the mirrors "on a primitive wooden mounting" he had used for taking the pictures. He explained, "I myself have no means for making a mounting, and therefore I would greatly appreciate an opportunity to mount a reflector, perhaps by attaching it to the tube of a telescope."

This letter was the beginning of a close friendship by mail between Bernhard Schmidt and Karl Schwarzschild, director of the Potsdam Observatory. During the next ten years Schwarzschild ordered mirror after mirror from Schmidt and was astounded at their perfection. The obscure young lens grinder with one arm had produced mirrors that surpassed in accuracy the largest and most expensive ones then used at Potsdam.

Meanwhile, with the money he made from the Potsdam mirrors, Schmidt was able to build himself an excellent telescope. It was not a giant, like the ones in professional observatories, but it allowed him to continue the photographic experiments that led to the first Schmidt camera. His telescope was a Cassegrainian reflector, named for a French professor who was a contemporary of Isaac Newton. Cassegrain had revised the Gregorian telescope, placing its eyepiece behind the primary mirror. This was much easier for an observer to reach than the customary side-view eyepiece, necessarily placed near the top of the tube on a Newtonian reflector.

With the help of this telescope—and later with an ingenious horizontal telescope—Schmidt took excellent pictures of the sun, the moon, and the planets. His fortunes were changing. At Potsdam, Schwarzschild had allowed Schmidt to refigure the curve and correct the grinding of the second largest mirror in the observatory—a 50-centimeter (about 19½ inches) reflector that had never been satisfactory. Everyone at the observatory was delighted with the result. The improved mirror was apparently flawless. If Schmidt could do the same kind of work on the observatory's largest mirror, a prized 80-centimeter objective, Schwarzschild felt that Potsdam would have the finest reflectors in the world. He set out to get a contract for Schmidt from the German government.

Only outstanding artistry [Schwarzschild wrote to the authorities in Berlin] can make an appreciable improvement in the 80-centimeter objective. My confidence in the quality of Schmidt's work is based not only on his artistry, but also on his extraordinarily clear insight into the mathematical principles of telescopic optics, which he as a self-trained man has developed for himself. Moreover, there is a much greater prospect for an early completion of the job. This is because Mr. Schmidt is an independent man who puts his entire energy into his work without relying on outside help.

But Schwarzschild had not taken into account the feelings of the original manufacturer. Rudolf Steinheil, grandson of the physicist Carl August von Steinheil, who had discovered the process of silvering glass mirrors, had produced the 80-centimeter mirror in the family workshop. He objected strenuously to having it tampered with by a one-armed amateur. Steinheil wanted the contract for improving the mirror and told Schwarzschild he thought he should have it. Just as Bernhard Schmidt was preparing to tackle the job, the German government intervened.

Like a defense attorney arguing for his client, Schwarzschild made one more plea in Schmidt's behalf. "Objectives are works of art," he argued, "and should be compared with works of art. There is the same difference between a Rembrandt painting and a painting from the school of Rembrandt as there is between an objective made by a master and an objective that comes out of a [commercial] workshop."

Schwarzschild's eloquence was ignored in Berlin and the contract went to Steinheil. The decision may have involved no more than the manufacturer's professional pride, but perhaps it was influenced by the discovery that Bernhard Schmidt, an Estonian, was an "enemy alien."

In 1914 Germany was at war and Estonia was on the other side, allied with its large neighbor, Russia. Schmidt, with his

solitary ways and strange, all-night activities, was under sus-
picion. Police came to his workshop in Mittweida to search
for evidence against him. When they saw the horizontal
telescope with its variety of mirrors, they were convinced
that it was a device for flashing light signals to Russian aircraft. Bernhard Schmidt was packed off to prison camp with
other "enemy aliens."

By 1916 Schmidt was back in Mittweida, out of prison but
allowed to work only under police surveillance. Making a living was not easy. His friend Karl Schwarzschild had been
killed in the war. Although he continued to correspond with
Potsdam through the observatory's new director, Hermann
Vogel, there was little work for him to do. Even if the observatory had wanted to order new mirrors from him, they
could not afford to pay for them. Germany was then pouring
all of its money into the war.

In spite of·the unwelcome visits by the police to his workshop and outdoor observatory, Schmidt continued to experiment with sky photography. The pictures he produced were
outstanding enough to bolster his confidence. On March 12,
1916, he decided to write to the Hamburg Observatory at
Bergedorf, enclosing some of his best photographs: "Allow
me to send you some astronomical photographs that I have
recently taken here at Mittweida. . . . Also let me ask
whether you perhaps have astronomical optics to be re-
figured, old object glasses or the like."

Professor Richard Schorr, then director of the Hamburg
Observatory, read the letter with interest, and studied the
photographs with even more interest. In October Schmidt
received an order from Schorr to build a telescope for the
observatory—a horizontal telescope like the one he had

mounted at Mittweida. Two years later, when the telescope was ready to be installed, Bernhard Schmidt visited Bergedorf for the first time.

He was so warmly received and so encouraged by the opportunity to work in a major observatory that he might have settled there permanently, if the observatory had not been struggling through the financial crisis that affected all of Germany. Back in Mittweida the situation was no better. Schmidt's workshop had so little business coming in that he was living on credit. But Schmidt felt at home in Mittweida. When he was invited to emigrate to Holland, as some other non-German scientists and technicians were doing, he refused.

Your invitation to Holland is very kind [he replied] but I have no idea what use I would be to your country, as I could operate neither as a factory owner nor as an independent craftsman. Here in Germany, astronomy has dropped into the background, and since there is nothing special to do in astronomical optics, I have recently taken up periscope problems. With periscopes made on my plan for use in closed passenger planes to observe the ground beneath, I have obtained fields of view up to more than 100 degrees with images sharp to the edge.

Hoping his periscope would give him a new source of income, Schmidt applied for a patent on his invention and started negotiations with an aircraft manufacturer. But things didn't move fast enough to save Schmidt's workshop. There was not enough money to keep it going. By 1923 a runaway inflation had made German money almost worthless. After twenty years in Mittweida, Bernhard Schmidt went home to Estonia.

In January 1924 Schmidt wrote to Professor Schorr in Bergedorf:

When the dollar got to be worth more than a million paper marks, I felt that I had better get out of Germany. I would have had more opportunity there, but what could I have done with the worthless billions and trillions? But now, since the new marks seem to be remaining stable, I plan to return to Mittweida. I have gotten some foreign orders and must get back to Germany to fill them.

Full of hope, Schmidt returned to Mittweida early in 1925, but the orders never materialized. In April he wrote to Schorr that he was discouraged enough "to turn my whole stock into junk and sell it for old iron and charcoal, and then take up something new."

He was saved from any such drastic action when an amateur astronomer in Griefswald bought his horizontal reflector. Schmidt hated to part with his old friend, the tele scope he had used to take his favorite sky photographs, but he had to have money to keep going.

As he had threatened in his letter to Schorr, he did "take up something new." For a little more than a year Bernhard Schmidt turned away from optics and concerned himself with propellors for sailing ships, a study he called "windmill engineering." He devised an unusual propellor that enabled a ship to sail against the wind but he was unable to patent it.

"Nobody believes that I can sail against the wind," he wrote to Schorr. "People ridicule the idea as if it were perpetual motion. To go against the wind, I use a fast-running light wind turbine that drives a water propellor." His description of the invention was full of almost boyish enthusiasm. He had loved sailing since his boyhood on the island in the Gulf of Finland, and the enthusiasm stayed with him all his life.

His failure to patent the propellor may have led Schmidt back to his first interest, astronomical optics. He wrote to Schorr again, asking tentatively whether there was any work he could do in Bergedorf. Schorr replied warmly that Schmidt would be welcome there.

Late in 1926 Bernhard Schmidt arrived at Bergedorf and set up his workshop in the basement of the observatory's main building. As a volunteer staff member he was free to use the telescopes and other facilities of the observatory. At last Schmidt had the kind of equipment he had always dreamed about and had never been able to afford.

Dr. Schorr, unable to pay Schmidt a regular salary, gave him enough optical work to do on the side to pay his living expenses. However, Schorr encouraged Schmidt's experiments and inventions, and he respected Schmidt's need for solitude and time to work on them.

Some of the other members of the staff didn't know quite what to make of Bernhard Schmidt. He was not at all gregarious—or even friendly—and he made it clear that he did not welcome visitors to his workshop.

"Only one man alone is worth anything," he told one of his colleagues. "Put two men together and they quarrel. A hundred of them make a rabble, and if there are a thousand or more they'll start a war." But in spite of this attitude, he did make friends at Bergedorf.

Dr. A. A. Wachmann, a staff astronomer who became

Schmidt's friend, was one of the few men privileged to visit the basement workshop. Twenty years after Schmidt's death, Wachmann remembered:

A glance into his workshop in the basement of the main building would reveal not only his industry but his genius at getting astounding results from apparently primitive means. Few people managed to enter there, where he worked at any hour of the day or night. If, however, he accepted you, and if you were content to watch in silence as you smoked, then you saw the true artist at work, served by a workshop of whose peculiarities he was fully master.

You would watch his steady concentration upon the piece he was working, and you would be astonished by the almost uncanny certainty with which he always knew the right moment to break off polishing to test the optical surface . . . You would wonder at the delicacy of touch of his left hand, the only one he had. Schmidt himself said, "My hand is more sensitive than the finest gauge," and when someone during his absence had playfully given the polishing tool a few strokes, he said at once, "Somebody has been fooling around with this."

At one time Dr. Schorr suggested that Schmidt take a few pupils into his workshop, but the solitary artist resisted the idea. Just as vehemently, he resisted the suggestion that he write down his methods and findings for others to study. "Let others collect experience for themselves," he said. "If I were to write it down, it would so shock the astronomers and opticians that I'd probably never get another order to construct anything."

Because he left no written records of his procedures—no accounts of false starts abandoned or of trial-and-error progress—nobody knows exactly how Bernhard Schmidt arrived at his great invention, the coma-free telescope camera. Astronomers saw the results soon after the first Schmidt camera was mounted at the Hamburg Observatory in 1931.

This remarkable telescope could do what no other had been able to do: it combined sharp images, powerful light-gathering, and wide field without any haziness or other distortions. Haziness, especially around the edges of an image, had been accepted as a necessary evil in any telescope with a wide field of view, because light rays passing through different areas of a lens—or reflected from different areas of a curved mirror—were focused at different points. Now Schmidt had found a way to eliminate the haze.

As Isaac Newton had done, Schmidt used a concave spherical mirror to receive the image. But between the front end of the tube and the mirror he placed a correcting lens, to bend the incoming light rays into a parallel path toward the mirror. This allowed the rays to bounce back to a single focus.

Facing the mirror, he placed a photographic plate to capture the reflection of the corrected image. If he had used an ordinary flat photographic plate, the resulting picture would have been distorted by the curve of the mirror, but Schmidt devised a spherical form, corresponding to the curve of the mirror, over which he fitted the photographic film. The result was a clear sharp picture.

Schmidt's sky photographs were praised in the world's observatories, but astronomers heard little about the inventor. The actions of world leaders and politicians, who had never heard of Bernhard Schmidt, intervened to keep him obscure for the rest of his life. He never received a single final order for his sky camera.

Schmidt's first telescope-camera was completed at the Hamburg Observatory in 1931, four years before the inventor's death.

When Adolph Hitler became Chancellor of Germany in August 1934, Schmidt's adopted country was losing friends all over the world. Foreign observatories were not likely to buy expensive equipment from Germany. A tentative order for a Schmidt telescope-camera came from Russia, but was canceled. German observatories couldn't afford to make any major purchases, since most of the government's money was being spent on the German military machine.

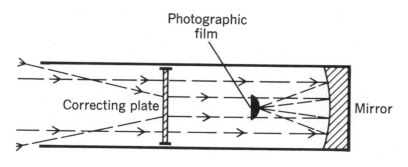

Schmidt's Telescope-Camera

If Bernhard Schmidt had lived a few years longer he would have seen the fame of his invention spread around the world. But on December 1, 1935, in the words of his friend Dr. Wachmann, "death took the polishing tool from his hands."

The following year, just before the outbreak of World War II, Dr. Schorr released the secret of Schmidt's curved photographic plate and correcting lens. Soon the Schmidt telescope-camera became standard equipment in many major observatories. In the United States the Palomar Observatory had one built with a 26-inch mirror, enlarging Schmidt's original design, which called for a 17-inch mirror. Other observatories began to build even larger ones. Harvard constructed one with a 33-inch mirror and a 24-inch correcting lens. In Cleveland, the Warner and Swasey Observatory had one with a 36-inch mirror and a 24-inch correcting plate.

In 1938 the Observatory Council of the California Institute of Technology decided to give the Palomar Observatory the largest Schmidt camera ever built, as a companion for the 200-inch Hale Telescope. Ten years later the Big Schmidt was completed—a giant camera with a 72-inch mirror and a 48-inch correcting plate.

At the same time in Germany, at the Hamburg Observatory, Bernhard Schmidt's former colleagues were trying to raise enough money to build their own Schmidt telescope. In 1949, while the Big Schmidt at Palomar was beginning its seven-year photographic marathon, the Hamburg astronomers were able to start their project with a government grant. On August 19, 1955, a new Schmidt camera was dedicated at the Hamburg Observatory before an international

The "Big Schmidt" telescope-camera at Mount Palomar.

gathering of astronomers who had come to honor the one-armed inventor.

Today research astronomy has become almost entirely a photographic science. Without the sensitive emulsion of photographic film, astronomers could never have seen much of the universe that is now familiar territory for them. The Schmidt telescope-camera extends their vision millions of light-years into space.

9

GROTE REBER'S
LISTENING TELESCOPE

Traditional astronomers paid little attention in 1933 to a
report that radio signals had been detected coming from the
center of the Milky Way. In their mountain monasteries,
the astronomers would soon be well equipped with telescopes and cameras to help them *see* the stars. But they had
no telescope for *listening* to the stars—until a young radio
amateur named Grote Reber invented one in 1937.

The first report of radio signals from the stars was made
by Karl Jansky at Bell Telephone Laboratories in New
Jersey. He was just twenty-three in 1928 when he came out
of the University of Wisconsin and went to work for Bell.
His first assignment was to investigate the static that was
interfering with the new transatlantic telephones. If he
could find out where the static came from, Bell engineers
might find a way to block it out.

After puzzling over the problem for a while, Jansky rigged
up an antenna in a New Jersey potato field, determined to
track down the source of the noise. His antenna, a strange
contraption made of pipes and wires, looked like a series of
metal goal posts lined up on a wooden frame. The whole

188

Grote Reber (1911–   ).

thing was mounted on wheels from an old Model-T Ford and could be turned on a circular track, to pick up signals from various directions.

With earphones attached to this "merry-go-round," Jansky was able to sweep the sky, as Herschel had done with his telescopes. But Jansky, not concerned with the stars, did his sweeping in the daytime as well as at night, listening to the noises picked up by his antenna. After a while he was able to account for some of the telephone static. It was easy enough to recognize the disturbances caused by thunderstorms, electric power lines, or commercial radio transmitters, but there was also a different kind of static. It was a faint persistent hissing—like the sound of bacon frying. Jansky couldn't explain it, but he was determined to find the source.

Karl Jansky's "merry-go-round" antenna, built in a New Jersey swamp to detect telephone static, picked up signals from the stars.

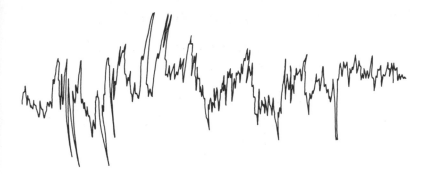

Recording of a Radio Source

After several months of listening Jansky began to think the hissing might come from the sun. The sound gradually grew louder during the day until it reached a peak, then gradually faded. There seemed to be a pattern in the sound. It seemed to move across the sky, as the sun did, from east to west.

Jansky made a recording device—a roll of paper moving slowly across the point of a pen attached to a meter. As radio signals entered the antenna, they were transformed into electrical impulses and fed into the meter. The pen, acting like the needle of an ordinary electric meter, moved a little or a lot, depending upon the intensity of the signal. The result on the roll of paper was a line that was almost straight when the signals were faint, rising to jagged points when the signals were intense.

As he studied the pattern, Jansky soon realized that the peak of the hissing did not come every day at the same time. It moved ahead of the sun, coming about four minutes earlier each day, until it was loudest at midnight when the sun was nowhere in sight. Obviously, the hissing did not come from the sun. Gradually, after several months, it "caught up" with the sun, always gaining four minutes a day.

Those four minutes were significant. Karl Jansky knew enough about astronomy to recognize the difference between the *solar day* (the time it takes the earth to rotate on its axis with respect to the sun), twenty-four hours, and the *sidereal day* (the time it takes the earth to rotate with respect to the stars), twenty-three hours and fifty-six minutes—a difference of exactly four minutes. This mysterious hissing, which reached its peak every twenty-three hours and fifty-six minutes, must come from beyond the solar system—from somewhere among the stars.

Jansky made his discovery in 1931. He said nothing about it publicly until after he had spent two more years experimenting—patiently gathering enough data to make a formal report. His first paper appeared in the *Proceedings of the Institute of Radio Engineers*. Even then, his report was read chiefly by radio men. Then, on May 4, 1933, Karl Jansky delivered a paper to the International Scientific Radio Union in Washington.

Suddenly Jansky found himself pursued by newspaper reporters who wanted to know more about his mysterious signals from the sky. To some of these people his report sounded like science fiction. Could this mean, a reporter asked, that somebody—or something—"out there" was trying to send a message to the earth? Jansky tried to squelch any such sensational interpretation of what he had found.

"There is no indication of any kind," he told reporters, "that these galactic waves constitute some kind of interstellar signaling or that they are the result of some form of intelligence striving for intragalactic communication." But

NEW RADIO WAVES TRACED TO CENTRE OF THE MILKY WAY

Mysterious Static, Reported by K. G. Jansky, Held to Differ From Cosmic Ray.

DIRECTION IS UNCHANGING

Recorded and Tested for More Than Year to Identify It as From Earth's Galaxy.

ITS INTENSITY IS LOW

Only Delicate Receiver Is Able to Register—No Evidence of Interstellar Signaling.

Discovery of mysterious radio waves which appear to come from the centre of the Milky Way galaxy was announced yesterday by the Bell Telephone Laboratories. The discovery was made during research studies on static by Karl G. Jansky of the radio research department at Holmdel, N. J., and

Flier Asks Blame in Crash, But Inquest Absolves Him

By The Canadian Press.

LONDON, May 4.—A chivalrous attempt to assume responsibility for the fatal crash of a Royal Air Force plane on May 1, in which Viscount Knebworth, pilot, and Aircraftman Harrison lost their lives, was made by Flight Lieutenant Eric Hobson at the inquest today. Despite Lieutenant Hobson's action, a verdict of "death due to misadventure" was returned.

Lieutenant Hobson, the leader of the section of which Lord Knebworth was a member, described how he unaccountably lost his height and at the end of a 2,000-foot dive got dangerously near the ground.

"The error in judgment was certainly not due to carelessness or recklessness," said Lieutenant Hobson, adding that Lord Knebworth was "absolutely blameless for what had happened, but had simply followed him according to orders."

KIDNAPPERS URGED TO ANSWER PLEAS

New Yorker Named to Act as Secret Agent for Return of McMath Child.

Radio waves from space were front-page news in 1933.

in spite of Jansky's firm denials, his report touched off wild speculations among science fiction enthusiasts.

A radio network persuaded Jansky to participate in a special fifteen-minute broadcast on May 15, 1933. The broadcast was sandwiched in between two comedy shows on WJZ in New York and was listed as "Radio from the Stars." That night at 8:30, New York time, former federal Radio Commissioner O. H. Caldwell introduced Karl Jansky to a national audience. The commentator promised a broadcast

that will break all records for long distance. We shall let the radio audience hear radio impulses picked up from somewhere outside the solar system, from somewhere among the stars. . . . Now, through the courtesy of the American Telephone and Telegraph Company, I will let you listen in on the sensitive receiving set at Holmdel, New Jersey, fifty miles southwest of New York City. Mixed in with the static, you will hear the hiss of radio waves from the stars.

Then the audience heard ten seconds of hissing. *The New York Times* said the next day that it "sounded like steam escaping from a radiator." That was all there was to it. Those who had expected some sensational other-worldly message were disappointed. But in Wheaton, Illinois, a twenty-two-year-old radio amateur listened to the broadcast and found it fascinating. Grote Reber had read Jansky's paper in the *Proceedings of the Institute of Radio Engineers*. Now he made up his mind to receive his own signals from the stars.

At twenty-two Grote Reber was a student at the Illinois Institute of Technology in Chicago. He lived with his parents, Schuyler and Harriet Reber, in nearby Wheaton, where he had been born on December 22, 1911. As a teenager he filled the family basement with radio equipment. At fifteen he built a shortwave transmitter and receiver and became a licensed radio amateur, with the call letters W9GFZ. The walls of his workshop were covered with cards he received from other "hams" around the world—radio buffs with whom he had communicated in code.

After the Jansky broadcast young Reber set to work on his own radio receiver for star signals. At first he tried adapting his shortwave radio equipment to tune in on very high frequencies, but something was wrong. He detected no mysterious hissing. Reber wrote to Jansky about his experiments and the two young men carried on a brief correspondence.

By 1935 Grote Reber was out of school and working for a radio company in Chicago, designing home receiving sets. While working at his drawing board, diagraming circuits for conventional radios, he found himself toying with another kind of design. What kind of circuitry would be most efficient for receiving signals from the Milky Way? What kind of shape would be best for such a receiver? How big would it have to be?

On an impulse he wrote to Jansky and asked if Bell Laboratories intended to do more research in the field of stellar radio. At the time he intended to apply for a job at Bell, but Jansky's reply changed his mind. The experiments with his "merry-go-round" receiver were over, Jansky said. He was already at work on a new assignment that had nothing to do with signals from the stars.

"I realized I had a clear field," Reber recalled later. "Nobody else was working on this problem. Anything I could discover was bound to be new."

Like any other explorer bound for unknown territory, he began to assemble his equipment. First he designed a new kind of antenna. Taking a hint from the optical astronomers, he decided to make it bowl-shaped. Astronomers at Mount Wilson used concave mirrors to collect light from the stars and bring it to a focus. Why couldn't he build a concave reflector to gather and focus radio waves? He wanted to make it as large as he could. If a large telescope mirror gathers four times as much light as one with half its diameter, a large radio mirror would gather more radio energy than a small one.

By the summer of 1937 the Rebers' back yard in Wheaton was full of construction materials. The young inventor had drawn blueprints for a huge bowl-shaped reflector, thirty-one feet in diameter. It was to be made of galvanized sheet iron, cut into forty-five wedge-shaped pieces fitted together like slices of pie. This big dish would have a small radio tower rising out of its center. Radio signals striking the reflecting surface of the bowl would bounce toward a single focus, about halfway up the tower. At this point Reber would place an aerial to capture the signals and feed them into a wideband high-frequency receiver, then into the basement control room where a meter would show him what was happening.

Before winter drove him indoors, Reber finished building his apparatus and mounted it on a movable wooden scaffolding. The bowl could be tilted and rotated, like a telescope, to explore the sky. Nearly a year later, in October 1938, he received his first signals from outer space.

After working all day at the radio company in Chicago he had come home to supper, then napped until midnight. It was all the sleep he would get that night. Just after midnight he went to the basement, put on his earphones, and watched the meter needle jump occasionally as cosmic static passed across his outdoor antenna. As he turned the tuning knob and adjusted the volume, he heard a steady uninterrupted hissing—just the way it had sounded five years earlier when the network had broadcast Jansky's "signals from the stars."

Reber picked up a pen and began jotting down meter readings in a notebook. Timing the signals with his watch, he entered a reading every minute. Before he knew it, the night was over. At 6:00 A.M. it was time to drive twenty-five miles to work. After that, such all-night vigils became routine.

Carefully, painstakingly, Grote Reber swept the Milky Way with his 31-foot electronic ear. As he surveyed the sky, he noticed that the signals from certain regions were especially strong. They were steady signals that did not fade or waver. When he tried to pin down their location he made a surprising discovery. These strong signals did not come from bright stars, as he had expected. They didn't even come from *visible* stars.

No concentrated beams of radio energy come from the visible stars [he wrote a few years later in *Scientific American*]. But there are certain small spots in the Milky Way that do yield intense radiation. No bright stars are present to account for it. The small spots are tiny enough to be considered "radio stars." Though invisible to us, they represent powerful concentrations of energy, like visible stars.

In Grote Reber's basement workshop a new science was born. From 1938 until after World War II Reber was virtually the only radio astronomer in the world. The term was unknown in the world's great observatories, where astronomers had not yet recognized the powerful tool created for them in Wheaton, Illinois.

While the war was going on, a few scientists were making nonmilitary experiments with a technique called *radar*, an abbreviation of Radio Detecting And Ranging. As early as the 1920's physicists had recognized that radio waves could be reflected, or bounced off, solid objects. At the United States Naval Research Laboratory in Washington, A. H. Taylor and L. C. Young devised a way to catch bouncing radio waves as they returned toward their source. From their own transmitter these men sent out high-frequency, short-wave radio signals, received the "echoes," and analyzed them. Soon they were able to recognize patterns identifying ships passing on the Potomac River. Eventually this technique became known as *radar*.

During World War II radar was used to detect enemy planes and battleships. A few scientists realized that it might have valuable peacetime uses as well. In 1942 a British physicist, J. Stanley Hey, designed a radar set to track German V-2 missiles being fired at England. Using this device, Hey became the first man to detect radio emissions from the sun. About the same time, these solar signals were also detected by an American, G. C. Southworth of Bell Laboratories, one of Jansky's colleagues. A few months later, Grote Reber independently identified the same signals with his pie-plate antenna.

After the war ended Hey built his own radio antenna, using secondhand parts from military radar, and detected the galactic hissing that Jansky had heard fifteen years earlier. Continuing his experiments, Hey discovered a sharply defined radio source where there was no visible star. He called it "Cygnus A," the first "radio star" ever catalogued.

With the discovery of Cygnus A, optical astronomers began to pay more attention to this new work being done by "communications" scientists. Suddenly, the science of radio astronomy grew up. Men at Palomar and Wilson began to compare notes with their listening brothers. Together they tracked down the sources of the strongest radio signals and found that most of them seemed to come from colliding galaxies or from gas clouds of exploded supernovae, such as the Crab nebula. Cygnus A, they discovered, was not a star, but a distant pair of galaxies in collision. Twenty years later it would be studied as the source of other strange radiation.

In November 1947 the National Bureau of Standards invited Grote Reber to come to Washington. The Bureau added that it would like to have his radio telescope moved to its experimental station in Sterling, Virginia. So Reber dismantled his treasure, packed up the pieces, and headed east.

The following year, while working in Washington as chief of the Experimental Microwave Research Section at the Bureau of Standards, Reber occasionally saw Karl Jansky at meetings of communications scientists. Jansky was intensely interested in Reber's work. His own experiments in radio astronomy had ended more than ten years earlier. He had presented his final paper, summarizing his work in the field, in April 1937 at a meeting of the Institute of Radio Engineers. After that he had been occupied with other problems. He told Reber that his colleagues at Bell Laboratories had been interested in his findings, but not enthusiastic enough to carry them further.

"As he explained it to me one time," Reber said, "the electrical engineers were not interested because they didn't know any astronomy and couldn't find anything useful in the subject. The astronomers were not interested because they didn't know any electrical engineering and considered their present techniques adequate for the study of the universe."

By the time the astronomers became interested, Jansky was too involved in other work—and too ill—to take up his research again. His health had been failing since he had left college, knowing he had a chronic kidney ailment. Now he suffered from high blood pressure and had to live very carefully. He was only forty-four when he died, in 1949, of a severe stroke.

Grote Reber spent four years with the Bureau of Standards in Washington, but he was restless. The work he was doing seemed routine and he was eager to try something new in his exploration of the sky. In the summer of 1951, with a grant from the Research Corporation of New York, he went to Hawaii, leaving his precious radio telescope in Virginia.

On top of Haleakala, an extinct volcano on the island of Maui, Reber started building a new radio telescope. At an altitude of ten thousand feet he had an unbroken view of the surrounding islands, the sea, and the horizon. When the weather was cloudy he was above the clouds. He lived alone in a cottage about halfway up the mountain and worked with some Portuguese laborers who helped him build his apparatus.

Earlier, back in Wheaton, Reber had mapped the sky with a receiver tuned to high-frequency, shortwave radiations. This time, from his volcanic peak, he intended to investigate low-frequency, long-wave radiations, beginning with waves from six to fifteen yards long.

All radio waves, short and long, are part of a much broader range of radiations, the *electromagnetic spectrum* of every kind of radiation yet discovered. All these electromagnetic waves travel at the same speed—186,000 miles per second. This is the speed of light, and light is just one kind of electromagnetic radiation. Each kind travels in a characteristic wave pattern, distinguishable by its *wavelength* or *frequency*.

Wavelength and frequency are two ways of describing the same characteristic of electromagnetic waves. Wavelength is a measure of the distance between one wave crest and the next. Frequency indicates the number of crests passing a given point in a second. If you multiply the frequency by the wavelength, the product is the velocity of light—186,000 miles per second.

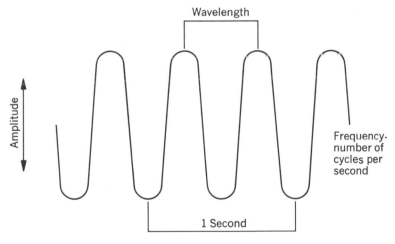

Wavelength and Frequency

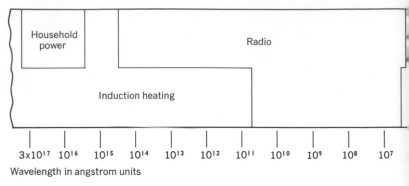

3×10^{17}	10^{16}	10^{15}	10^{14}	10^{13}	10^{12}	10^{11}	10^{10}	10^{9}	10^{8}	10^{7}

Wavelength in angstrom units

The Electromagnetic Spectrum

If the known electromagnetic spectrum could be diagramed in a 12-inch space, the part that can be seen by the human eye would occupy only about one-eighth of an inch. This "visible light" spectrum, with all its colors, is approximately in the middle of the diagram. On one side of it, the electromagnetic waves range from the very low-frequency (long) ones of household electric power, radio, and heat to the infrared waves. On the other side, they range from ultraviolet radiation, X-rays, and gamma rays to cosmic rays and the mysterious unknown high-frequency radiations beyond.

Long waves can be measured from crest to crest in standard units like feet, yards, meters, and even miles. Very short waves travel so rapidly from crest to crest that a special unit of measurement was adopted—the *angstrom* unit, named for a nineteenth-century Swedish physicist, Anders Jonas Ångström. One angstrom is one hundred-millionth (1/100,000,000) of a centimeter, indicated by the symbol Å. Wavelength is represented by the symbol λ. The expression λ = 6,000 Å means a wavelength of 6,000 angstroms, in the red range of visible light.

202

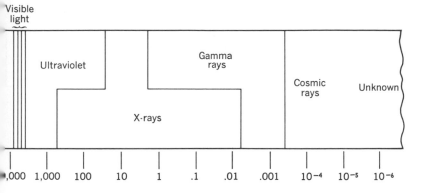

Visible light

| Ultraviolet | | Gamma rays | | Cosmic rays | Unknown |

X-rays

| ,000 | 1,000 | 100 | 10 | 1 | .1 | .01 | .001 | 10^{-4} | 10^{-5} | 10^{-6} |

Some electromagnetic waves cannot pass through the earth's atmosphere, just as visible light is unable to shine through a brick wall. One part of the upper atmosphere, the ionosphere, is made up of electrified particles that make it particularly difficult for long radio waves to pass through. This is a good thing for radio broadcasting on earth. When signals from a commercial radio transmitter hit the ionosphere, they bounce back to receivers on earth. Without the ionosphere, the signals would keep traveling indefinitely into space.

If there were a radio transmitter on Mars sending out signals of ordinary commercial wavelength, the signals would never reach earthbound receivers. The ionosphere would keep them out, bouncing them back into space. Some radio waves, however, can get through the ionosphere. Those with wavelengths of about one centimeter to ten meters do come through. Radio scientists call the part of the spectrum that contains these wavelengths a "radio window." Radiations in this range are picked up by radio telescopes.

With his telescope on top of a Hawaiian volcano, Grote

Reber first tried to capture some of the longest of these waves—six to fifteen yards long. From the beginning he ran into trouble. During the day the sun emitted electrified particles interfering with his reception. At night, even though he was above the weather, there were electrical storms in the upper atmosphere to distort the long waves he was trying to pick up. When he found no significant long waves, he looked for shorter wavelengths of about three yards. At this frequency, he succeeded in detecting several intense radio sources to add to his map of the sky.

After three years in Hawaii, Reber began to look toward new horizons. Several years earlier he had written:

We do not know much about galactic radio waves in the Southern Hemisphere because few experiments have been conducted there. Yet this region is one of the most interesting, for some of the brightest and darkest spots of the Milky Way are visible there. Moreover, in that location the center of the Milky Way is high in the sky.

Grote Reber was free to go wherever he liked. Why shouldn't he take a look at these interesting regions of the Milky Way? By this time, the picture had changed; *many* experiments were being conducted in Australia. Australian scientists had embraced radio astronomy with enthusiasm and were building ingenious radio telescopes quite different from Reber's dish-shaped original. Some had corkscrew-shaped antennae. Others were formed like crescents. So, in 1954, Reber decided to see for himself what the Australians were doing. He went to Tasmania, where he worked for several years with the Commonwealth Scientific and Industrial Research Organization.

While Reber was in Australia, the world's largest radio telescope was being built. A 250-foot version of Reber's big dish was completed in 1957 at Jodrell Bank, near Cambridge, England. In the United States a smaller one, 140 feet in diameter, was being built at the brand-new National Radio Astronomy Observatory at Green Bank, West Virginia. Plans were already in the works for a 600-foot "ear" to be built in a valley near Sugar Grove, not far from Green Bank.

Late in 1957 Grote Reber was in Hawaii again, winding up his observations from Haleakala, when he received an invitation from the National Radio Astronomy Observatory to come to Green Bank. A few weeks later he returned to the United States.

When he arrived at Green Bank, Reber found the pieces of his original radio telescope waiting to be assembled. For the third time he began to build his 31-foot reflector, this time on the left side of the front entrance to the new radio observatory. The astronomers at Green Bank wanted to keep it there as a permanent monument.

From the men at Green Bank, Reber learned that his apparatus had done some traveling since he had left it in Sterling, Virginia. Soon after he had gone to Hawaii, the Bureau of Standards had closed the experimental station at Sterling. Some of the staff scientists were sent to a new station in Boulder, Colorado. Before they left, they had Reber's telescope dismantled and shipped to Boulder, but when the pieces arrived nobody knew how to put it together. Finally, the pieces were simply left to gather dust for several years until the National Radio Astronomy Observatory sent for them.

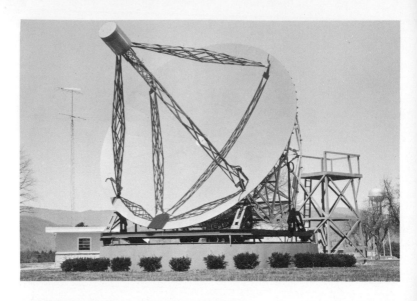

The 140-foot rotatable radio telescope at the National Radio Astronomy Observatory, Green Bank, West Virginia (*below*) has the same "big dish" design as Reber's first radio telescope (*above*) which now stands at the observatory's entrance.

While reassembling his telescope on a grassy plot about a hundred feet away from the front entrance to the observatory, Reber had an idea. If his radio telescope had become a museum piece, surely Jansky's ingenious "merry-go-round" antenna deserved equal attention. There was room on the right side of the entrance for Jansky's apparatus.

Reber found out from Bell Laboratories that Jansky's original had been destroyed long ago. With the help of G. C. Southworth, a retired Bell scientist who had worked with Jansky, Reber tracked down other men who remembered details of the experiments in the potato field, nearly thirty years before. Jansky's original gear box had been preserved. Now it could be used again in a replica of the "merry-go-round." Responding to Reber's enthusiasm, Bell engineers set out to build an accurate replica of Jansky's antenna.

Most of the parts were easy enough to find, but the wheels and axles from Model-T Fords, used by Jansky in the original, were scarce. In 1959 few Model T's were left. Reber made the rounds of junk yards and advertised in West Virginia newspapers until he found enough wheels.

Today, when visitors enter the gate of the National Radio Astronomy Observatory, they see both historic instruments —one on either side of the road.

In 1961 Grote Reber returned to Tasmania to continue the studies he had begun earlier. He and his Australian colleagues became the first radio astronomers to compile detailed information about low-frequency radiations from space, at a wavelength of 144 meters. Reber came home to the United States in May 1967 and prepared a report of what he and his colleagues had found. It was first published in the *Journal of the Franklin Institute* in January 1968.

Once his report was completed Reber was ready to look for another challenge. At fifty-six he had lost none of the eagerness and curiosity that led him to build the world's first radio telescope. Interviewed in New York late in 1967, Reber talked with enthusiasm about the past. When asked about his future plans, he only smiled. "I'm looking around for a project," he answered. At the Research Corporation in New York, the foundation that sponsored several of his projects, an acquaintance said, "He isn't likely to talk much about what he's doing until he has done it."

In the thirty-five years since he heard the network broadcast of Karl Jansky's hissing signals from the stars, Grote Reber has seen a complex science grow out of the questions he asked himself in Wheaton, Illinois. In the early 1940's he was the only radio astronomer in the world, searching the sky with the only radio telescope. Now, in many countries of the world, there are hundreds of scientists working with magnified versions of Reber's bowl-shaped antenna, seeking answers to questions that multiply year by year.

Some of these questions have brought radio astronomers and optical astronomers into close collaboration. The biggest joint search for truth about the universe began in 1961, soon after Palomar astronomer Allan R. Sandage announced his discovery of a strange, starlike object in the place where Cambridge radio astronomers had located a strong radio source.

The object was called simply 3C-48 (the forty-eighth source in the third *Cambridge Catalogue of Radio Sources*). Photographs taken with the 200-inch telescope revealed a faint bluish star, but Sandage was puzzled by the lines revealed by the spectrograph. They were unlike the spectrum of any other star he had ever seen. He reported that he could not account for them.

By 1963 four more radio sources had been identified with starlike objects—not galaxies or supernovae, but concentrated sources of energy that seemed to be stars, yet were not quite like stars. They became known as *quasars* (quasi-stellar radio sources), a brand-new challenge for astronomers.

Palomar astronomer Maarten Schmidt patiently studied the spectrum of a quasar designated 3C-273 and made some discoveries that shook the astronomers' previous notions about the makeup of the universe. According to Schmidt's calculations, 3C-273 was traveling away from the earth at tremendous speed—47,400 kilometers (about 29,000 miles) per second. If these calculations were correct, the object would have to be very far away—too far away to be visible even to the Hale telescope—*unless* it were more than a billion times bigger and brighter than the sun.

The fact that distant 3C-273 was even faintly visible to the 200-inch telescope seemed to indicate that it was the largest and brightest object ever detected by any kind of telescope—as if the mass of a whole galaxy were packed into a single object. Was it possible?

The world's astronomers, at radio telescopes and optical telescopes, set out to find out all they could about quasars—touching off debates over conflicting theories about them in scientific meetings and university lecture halls.

The hundreds of unanswered questions raised by the discovery of quasars led to plans for building more and bigger radio telescopes. The National Aeronautics and Space Administration orbited a radio telescope on an Explorer satel-

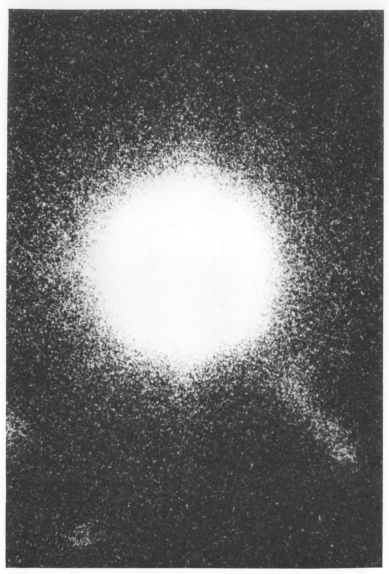

A strong radio source, quasar 3C-273, photographed by the 200-inch Hale telescope, is the subject of debate among astronomers.

lite in 1967. This organization already has plans for a radio telescope on the moon.

While committees meet and teams of astronomers are assembled, the inventor of the radio telescope continues to work alone, looking for more questions to explore. Grote Reber's invention has extended our penetration of the universe to about eight billion light-years away. Many astronomers believe that this is the outer limit of the observable universe—as far as we can go.

10

HERBERT FRIEDMAN'S
ROCKET TELESCOPES

In the summer of 1949 Palomar astronomers were completing their first year of sky mapping with the 200-inch Hale reflector, assisted by the Big Schmidt. That same year Karl Jansky died and Grote Reber was explaining the techniques of the new radio astronomy to communications scientists in Washington. In New Mexico, at the White Sands Missile Range, a soft-spoken young Brooklyn-born astrophysicist launched a new kind of astronomy—on a German V-2 rocket.

This astrophysicist, Dr. Herbert Friedman of the United States Naval Research Laboratory, was one of the first astronomers to carry his observations above the earth's atmosphere. The discoveries he made there led eventually, in 1962, to one of the biggest surprises of the Space Age—X-ray stars. These discrete (sharply defined) X-ray sources, as distinct as Reber's radio stars, opened up a brand-new dimension for astronomers to explore.

With his rocket-borne telescopes, Herbert Friedman founded X-ray astronomy, the study of celestial sources of X-rays. Within the first few years of its life, the infant science

212

Herbert Friedman (1916–   ).

almost outgrew the equipment that could be carried aloft on rockets. Looking ahead, Friedman began to plan large X-ray telescopes to travel in space aboard the Orbiting Astronomical Observatories to be launched in the 1970's by the National Aeronautics and Space Administration. As early as 1967 he had detailed plans for an X-ray observatory to be built on the moon. With these new tools he hoped to explore the outer limits of the universe.

Dr. Friedman denies that he "invented" rocket astronomy. "The idea of doing astronomy from rockets goes back a long way," he told an interviewer in 1967. "The Germans were thinking about it twenty-five or thirty-five years ago, but it wasn't until after the war, when the German V-2 rockets were brought to this country, that we thought seriously about sending up an instrument package on a rocket."

The V-2 rocket had been designed to carry a thousand-pound warhead. American engineers wanted to fire the rockets to test their propulsion systems, but they didn't want to carry warheads. Friedman and his colleagues at the Naval Research Laboratory proposed a payload of scientific instruments to fill the space designed for the explosives.

"Various groups put in their suggestions," Friedman said. "Some wanted to fly cosmic ray experiments. Others wanted to study the atmosphere at high altitudes. Biologists wanted to send living specimens into space. Astronomers wanted to study the sun.

"We chose the sun because it would be the easiest celestial body to study with the primitive instruments we had. We didn't put telescopes on those early rockets because there was no way to aim them at anything or to keep them stable. The rockets spun around so that any instruments we had would sweep over the sky at random. The sun was the brightest object in the sky—and the only one we could hope to catch on one of those spinning trips."

Here was the opportunity every astronomer dreamed of—a chance to forget about "windows" in the atmosphere, a chance to examine the whole electromagnetic spectrum of the sun beyond the narrow limits of visible light, even beyond the range of radio signals picked up by the radio telescopes. Above the confining atmosphere, where should an astronomer look first? Herbert Friedman decided to begin with the ultraviolet region of the sun's spectrum, where the wavelengths are shorter than those that pass through the atmosphere. A spectrograph was built into the earliest test rockets, but it ran into difficulty because it couldn't be aimed.

"There were at least three groups working on these early solar studies," Friedman recalled. "Besides the Naval Research Lab team, there was one from the Air Force and another from Johns Hopkins. While we were waiting for guidance systems to be developed, I thought we might be able to gather a lot of astrophysical information by sending up broad-band photometers—the kind used by ground-based astronomers to classify stars according to their colors.

"When we launched the photometers in 1949, they gave us the first quantitative measure of the sun's radiation in the extreme ultraviolet region—and of solar X-rays."

This was the beginning of Friedman's study of celestial X-rays. While continuing his measurements of X-rays and ultraviolet radiation from the sun, he occasionally picked up X-rays from other parts of the sky. The more he detected, the more curious he became. Finally he decided to pin the X-rays down, if possible, to clearly defined, discrete sources. For this, he needed a telescope.

In 1956 American rockets had progressed far beyond the relatively crude German V-2. The new rockets, designed to launch future satellites, carried sophisticated guidance systems that could be controlled from the ground. An Aerobee rocket, Friedman felt, was stable enough to carry a telescope aimed at some point beyond the solar system.

Designing a telescope to detect X-rays was no easy matter, Friedman discovered. A conventional reflecting telescope wouldn't do. Such a gently curved mirror would merely absorb the X-rays, except for a few that might glance off the surface. A telescope for detecting X-rays would have to have a special mirror—a long, deep, tapered cylinder of a mirror. To be effective, it would have to be large—much too large to ride on an Aerobee rocket.

While looking for solutions to the problems involved in building an X-ray telescope, Friedman and his colleagues tackled a simpler problem. An ordinary telescope could, they knew, detect ultraviolet rays. The team designed a 6-inch reflector, combined with photometers for recording ultraviolet radiation. It was the first telescope ever carried into space. When it was launched on an Aerobee rocket from White Sands in 1957, it picked up intense ultraviolet signals from hot blue stars. The more common yellow stars, like our sun, the scientists discovered, were not significant sources of ultraviolet rays.

In spite of the obstacles, Herbert Friedman refused to give up his study of celestial X-rays. If a conventional telescope could not give him the information he wanted, he would design something that could.

"It was the most primitive kind of telescope," he remembered. "Simply a bundle of tubes—like a bunch of drinking straws tied together—mounted in front of a sensitive Geiger counter, with mechanical baffles to limit the field of view." With this crude instrument he continued to search for X-ray sources in the sky. During 1957 and 1958 he detected a diffuse background of X-rays all around the sky, but no sharply defined source.

On October 4, 1957, the Soviet Union made history with the successful launching of Sputnik I, the first man-made satellite to orbit the earth. A month later, a larger Russian satellite, Sputnik II, carried a live dog into orbit. American scientists were badgered to "catch up with the Russians." Physicists, chemists, mathematicians, and astronomers were recruited for a gigantic space program, which was organized as the National Aeronautics and Space Administration.

The new organization found a ready-made nucleus for its team of scientists. The entire staff of Project Vanguard, then building an earth satellite to be launched by the United States in 1958, was recruited by NASA. Other scientists were transferred to NASA from the Naval Research Laboratory, where Herbert Friedman and his colleagues had already launched a small space program of their own.

Friedman himself was thousands of miles away from Washington when NASA was being organized. In the summer of 1958 he was aboard a ship in the South Pacific, 400 miles from Samoa, in the Danger Islands. With a shipload of scientific equipment, he was waiting for an eclipse of the sun, happy and satisfied to be doing exactly what he was doing. "It was an ivory tower situation," he recalled, "doing astronomy out there in the middle of the ocean. I was there

In the summer of 1958 Dr. Friedman was aboard a ship in the South Pacific, waiting for an eclipse of the sun. On one of his rockets he painted the names of his sons, Jon and Paul.

218

to study the solar eclipse using rocket-borne X-ray detectors."

"We wanted to know," he explained, "whether X-rays came from the full disc of the sun uniformly, or whether they came from certain active centers, like sunspots, or perhaps from far out in the corona. The eclipse gave us the opportunity we needed. As the moon moved across the face of the sun, we could examine small regions while others were blocked out."

Aboard the U.S.S. *Point Defiance*, a Navy vessel equipped as a floating launch pad and laboratory, Friedman and his staff had mounted six double-stage rockets, designed to carry their instruments 800,000 miles into the air. Five of the six rockets were fired on schedule, one after the other. During the brief period of the eclipse, less than two hours from beginning to end, the rocket-borne detectors recorded the information Friedman was seeking.

When it was analyzed, the data showed that most solar X-rays came from high in the corona, though sunspot areas were also strong sources. Ultraviolet rays, on the other hand, were completely blocked out during the few moments of total eclipse. This told the scientists that ultraviolet radiation came from a region close to the normally visible interior of the sun's disc, rather than from the corona, which was visible during the eclipse. An even more exciting discovery came to Friedman and his team as an unexpected bonus, because the sixth rocket aboard the *Point Defiance* refused to go off on time. When the balky rocket finally went up, the day after the eclipse, its flight coincided with the appearance of a towering solar flare, a phenomenon they could not have predicted. The flare, they discovered, emitted X-rays more intense than any other signals recorded during the eclipse.

When Herbert Friedman returned to Washington, he found that many of the men he had worked with at the Naval Research Laboratory had gone over to the new NASA organization. Their plans for the future were exciting and Friedman was interested in what they were doing, but for himself he chose the much smaller facilities of the Naval Research Lab. He had always preferred to work alone, most of the time. In a huge organization like NASA, he felt he might be swallowed up in vast projects, no longer free to pursue his research wherever it led him. Later Friedman participated in NASA projects—including the Orbiting Solar Observatories launched in 1965 and 1967—but that was long after his experiments at N.R.L. had led him deep into the unexpected mysteries of X-ray astronomy.

As Chief Scientist of the E. O. Hulburt Center for Space Research at the Naval Research Laboratory, Dr. Friedman directed many kinds of experiments in astrophysics and rocket or satellite astronomy, but he never deserted his individual quest for knowledge. There were questions he had to answer, and each answer he found brought more questions. Often the path of his research made unexpected turns.

"We continually change direction as we find new and exciting areas to explore," he said in 1967. "That is one of the attractions of N.R.L. Because we are small, we are flexible and able to change."

This flexibility has been characteristic of Herbert Friedman all his life. The son of Samuel and Rebecca Friedman, he was born in Brooklyn, New York, on June 21, 1916. His father, an art dealer, had a shop in Manhattan, near Greenwich Village. Young Herbert was fascinated by the paintings and sculptures in his home and in his father's shop. As a very young child he loved to draw and paint. His mother liked to tell friends about Herbert's "studio" under the dining room table, where he took his crayons and paper so that he could work undisturbed by his brother and sister.

Herbert made up his mind to become an artist. When he enrolled in Brooklyn College he planned his four-year course as an art student. Then, in his junior year, he discovered physics. It was a revelation that changed the direction of his life. At the end of his senior year he received his bachelor's degree in physics.

Jobs for young physicists were scarce in 1936 when Friedman came out of Brooklyn College, so he went to work as a commercial artist. Before the summer was over, he had won a physics scholarship to Johns Hopkins University. Now he put away his pencils and brushes and returned to the world of science. The next four years he filled with teaching, studying, supervising undergraduate laboratories, and completing a dissertation on solid state physics. From that time on, he was committed to science, though painting was still his hobby. Later, colleagues often recognized the hand of an artist in the experiments he devised.

After receiving his Ph.D. in 1940, Herbert Friedman married Gertrude Miller, a girl he had known since his undergraduate days in Brooklyn. For another year he stayed at Johns Hopkins as an instructor in physics. Then in 1941, shortly before the United States entered World War II, he joined the metallurgy division of the Naval Research Laboratory.

During the war Friedman became chief of the new electron optics branch of the laboratory. His ingenious use of X-ray reflections to speed up the precision cutting of quartz crystals, then being used in military radio transmitters, won him the Navy Distinguished Service Award in 1945. His invention, he was told, had saved at least fifty million man-hours of labor and had made possible the mass production of vital communications equipment. The Navy award was only one of a long list of honors and awards that were to come to this quiet, diligent scientist. Each new award, his colleagues said, found Herbert Friedman slightly surprised that his work had attracted public attention.

When the war ended Friedman was at work on a compact device for measuring radioactive fallout from atomic bombs. The devastating aftereffects of the bombs dropped on Hiroshima and Nagasaki were later studied by teams of scientists equipped with these detectors. For the next few years Friedman continued to work on radiation-testing devices —even after the Navy started its experiments with rockets.

In one of the first postwar experiments, with a Geiger counter riding a V-2 rocket, he made the first measurements of X-rays from the sun. These rays, locked outside the earth's atmosphere, had been inaccessible to George Ellery Hale, even with his spectroheliograph. Now Herbert Friedman sent his measuring device above the atmosphere to meet them.

During the next few years Friedman answered other questions about the sun, using equipment that gradually became more complex, launched aboard rockets that had been greatly improved since the primitive V-2. In 1956 he experimented briefly with "Rockoons," an ingenious combination of 12-foot rockets with 72-foot plastic balloons filled with helium. The Rockoons had been developed by Professor

James A. Van Allen of the State University of Iowa for cosmic ray research.

As a result of his Rockoon experiments Friedman made a surprising discovery. X-rays, he found, were responsible for radio fade-outs during solar flares. Scientists had previously assumed that ultraviolet rays were to blame. They knew that X-rays could not penetrate the atmosphere, but Friedman produced proof that solar flares sometimes generated X-rays intense enough to enter the ionosphere—the upper layer of atmosphere which absorbs some kinds of radio waves.

Friedman's study of X-rays from the sun occupied most of his time for the next few years, but he was adaptable enough to explore an occasional bypath. While preparing for the International Geophysical Year, 1957, he and his colleagues had sent up the first rocket-borne telescope, the ultraviolet detector. Then, with the primitive bundle of tubes bound to a Geiger counter—the first X-ray telescope—they had made their tentative search for X-ray sources among the stars. After that, other projects intervened and the X-ray work had to be set aside temporarily.

Other teams of scientists became interested in Friedman's X-ray discoveries and began their own experiments. In June 1962 one of these teams detected the first concentrated X-ray source outside the solar system. Riccardo Giacconi, Herbert Gursky, and F. R. Paolini of the American Science and Engineering Corporation, and Bruno B. Rossi of the Massachusetts Institute of Technology used wide-field Geiger counters on spinning rockets to survey a spiral strip of sky, including the moon. While looking for lunar X-rays, they discovered a strong source in the constellation Scorpius. They thought these X-rays might be coming from the very center of our galaxy. When they repeated the experiment in October, the center of the galaxy was below the horizon, out of the range of their instruments. They were unable to confirm their first discovery, but found two more possible concentrations of X-rays. A third experiment, in June 1963, again detected strong X-rays from Scorpius.

A few months earlier, in April 1963, Herbert Friedman and his colleagues at N.R.L. had launched another Aerobee rocket equipped with an X-ray counter ten times more sensitive than the detectors used by the other group, but it covered the same wavelength.

The N.R.L. scientists, Stuart Bowyer, Talbot A. Chubb, Edward T. Byram, and Dr. Friedman, deliberately slowed down the spin of their rocket so that it would wobble as it went up, slowly revolving and scanning almost all of the sky above the horizon. It swept over the Scorpius region eight times. Each time, the X-ray signal was detected, strong and clear.

When Friedman and his associates pinpointed the location of the X-ray source and looked it up on a map of the sky, they found no visible star. Like Reber's radio stars, this X-ray emitter seemed to be an invisible source of electromagnetic waves. Unlike Reber's discoveries, it did not emit radio waves. "It is comparable," Friedman wrote, "to that [X-radiation] emitted by the quiet sun in the same wavelength range. Yet the entire neighborhood around the source is devoid of any visibly bright star, nebulosity or radio emission."

"What kind of celestial object," he asked himself, "could produce such intense X-ray emission and still remain invisible in the optical and radio wavelengths?"

Dr. Friedman (*right*) and his colleague Edward T. Byram (*left*) filled the inside of an Aerobee rocket with X-ray detection devices.

Could it be a neutron star? Nobody had ever found a neutron star, but astronomers had been looking for one since 1934, when Walter Baade and Fritz Zwicky of the Mount Wilson Observatory proposed that such objects might exist. The idea appealed to J. Robert Oppenheimer and G. M. Volkoff, then at the University of California at Berkeley, who worked out a theory of the structure and evolution of neutron stars.

A neutron star, they theorized, would be all that remained if a very large star used up all its energy and collapsed. This remainder would be a highly condensed mass of neutrons—as much mass as our sun, for example, packed into a sphere ten miles in diameter. Its temperature would be tremendous, about ten million degrees Kelvin, and it would emit X-rays—at least ten billion times more X-rays than visible light.

Friedman's later experiments did not confirm the existence of a neutron star in Scorpius, but they did turn up more and more concentrated sources of X-rays. Here was a new branch of astronomy as challenging and promising as radio astronomy. Friedman and his team began a concentrated effort to locate and map X-ray sources in the universe.

By the end of 1964 they had detected and fixed the positions, to within a degree or two, of ten X-ray sources. One of these was the Crab nebula, the first visible X-ray source ever mapped. This was an exciting discovery for any astronomer. The legendary Crab nebula, first observed as a supernova by Chinese astronomers in 1054, later attracted the attention of Tycho Brahe and Johannes Kepler, who thought they had discovered a "new" star.

To find out what part of the expanding Crab nebula was the source of the X-rays, Friedman used a technique similar to the one he had used to study the sun during the eclipse of 1958. The moon was his tool. As the edge of the moon moved across the face of the Crab nebula, Friedman's detectors measured the X-rays emitted from each area of the nebula, from edge to center to edge. As the rim of the moon passed over the center of the Crab, the signals abruptly diminished, telling him that the source of the strongest X-rays was a small, sharply defined area at the very core of the nebula.

The catalogue of X-ray stars grew to thirty-seven in 1965. All but two of these were close to the plane of our galaxy, the Milky Way, and were presumed to be in this galaxy, like

The Crab nebula, probably first observed by Chinese astronomers in 1054, is the source of strong X-rays, detected by Dr. Friedman and his colleagues in 1964.

227

the Crab. But the other two were located higher up—perhaps outside the galaxy.

In the spring of 1966 the Naval Research Laboratory announced that Friedman and his team had pinpointed the two X-ray sources outside the Milky Way. Both of them coincided with strong radio sources—Stanley Hey's radio galaxy, Cygnus A, and the strong source in Virgo called M87. The X-rays from both these sources seemed to be from ten to a hundred times stronger than the energy they emitted in the radio wavelengths.

The most powerful X-ray source in Friedman's growing catalogue, discovered in 1967, was the mysterious quasar 3C-273. As an X-ray source the quasar was a *billion* times stronger than the Crab nebula and about five hundred times as strong as radio galaxy M87. The X-rays from this source were about fifty times as strong as its radio waves and about twice as intense as its visible light. In other words, this strange object could be studied as a visible object, a radio source, and an X-ray source—and the X-rays were strongest.

In another part of the electromagnetic spectrum, the infrared region, the radiations from 3C-273 were even more intense than the X-rays. Astronomers had first observed its infrared luminosity in 1965 and had found it a hundred times as intense as the visible brightness. During two years of observations they noticed that the infrared rays faded gradually until they were only ten times as strong as the visible light, but they were still stronger than the X-rays. This discovery led Herbert Friedman's imagination into a new path of research. This quasar—a visible star, a radio star, and an X-ray star—was also an infrared star. How many other discrete infrared sources were there in the heavens?

By the end of 1967 Friedman and his colleagues had developed a 5-inch telescope to be used in a search for discrete infrared sources in the sky. An earthbound telescope wouldn't work—since the earth's atmosphere locks out infrared rays coming from space. A few astronomers had sent balloon-borne telescopes above the atmosphere to study infrared radiations from the sun, moon, some planets, and several stars. Now Friedman's team planned a rocket-launched experiment.

"We're almost ready," he said in November 1967, "to send up our 5-inch infrared telescope. We will keep it cool throughout the flight—down to 4 degrees Kelvin (about −273 Centigrade)—with liquid helium. We are going to survey the sky to see if we can detect a background radiation which would support the 'big bang' theory of the origin of the universe."

Dr. Friedman referred to one of the three most popular present-day theories of how the universe began: the *big bang, oscillating,* and *steady state* theories. Some astronomers believe that the universe began in a single explosion—the "big bang"—and has been expanding for ten billion years. All the galaxies of the universe, these astronomers believe, are fragments of this great explosion, forever moving outward and away from each other. Other astronomers, supporters of the "oscillating universe," carry this idea a step further, theorizing that the expanding material from the big bang eventually contracts again, then explodes in another big bang, every eighty billion years, in a never ending cycle. "Steady state" believers claim that the universe has always existed and always will. As the galaxies move away from each other, these astronomers think, new galaxies are formed to fill in the gaps, keeping the amount of matter in the universe constant.

"This is such a fundamental question," said Herbert Friedman, "that we feel it is worth a tremendous effort to try to find the answer. We also have the intuitive feeling that once we succeed in observing in the infrared, we will be surprised by a lot of other things. It will open up—like X-ray astronomy and ultraviolet astronomy—with more surprises."

During the same 1967 interview Dr. Friedman looked to the future of X-ray astronomy and predicted that it would become an important part of the huge space astronomy program at NASA. "In the 1970's," he said, "if NASA goes ahead with present plans for observatories in orbit, we will have an X-ray telescope in space on a stable platform. From an orbiting observatory, we will be able to make constant observations instead of observing for a few minutes at a time, as we do from rockets. We could hope to map tens of thousands of X-ray sources. We could see things a thousand times weaker than the weakest we have detected so far. We may see even farther than the radio telescopes have seen, and they have already detected signals from eight billion light-years away."

A large reflecting telescope for gathering X-rays, now being studied by teams of astronomers, is to be launched by NASA in one of the Apollo projects of the 1970's. Sometime in the 1980's there may be a *manned* observatory in space carrying a 120-inch reflector, larger than the one at Mount Wilson.

Herbert Friedman is optimistic about the plans for such an observatory. "Most of the debate," he said, "has been over whether to put the 120-inch telescope on the moon or

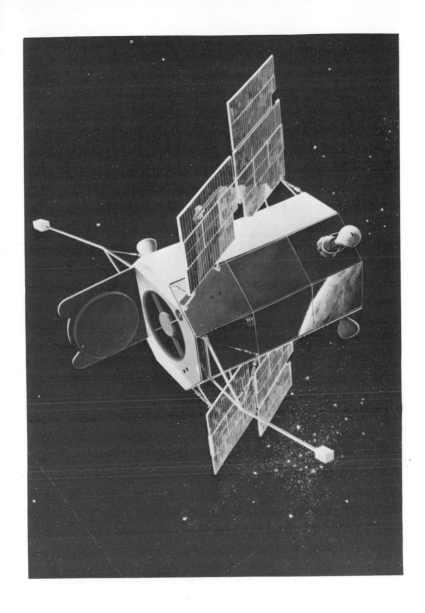

Artist's drawing shows NASA's first Orbiting Astronomical Observatory, launched in 1967. A power failure prevented any experiments.

into orbit. Consensus seems to be that such a large telescope should be in orbit. When NASA orbits this observatory, we [at N.R.L.] hope to be involved. But between now and then there is a lot to be done."

The future is full of exciting plans for Herbert Friedman. "We would like to orbit a very large X-ray detector—100 square feet. We've already built prototypes and know that it is feasible. If NASA tells us they can put it into orbit, we can go ahead and build the detector.

"There are other possibilities, too. I have proposed that we put an X-ray detector on the moon." Dr. Friedman's design for his moon observatory looks very different from that of an optical telescope. A network of crisscrossed wires on a flat frame, it looks more like a giant-sized tennis net. He talked about it with enthusiasm.

"The moon is an ideal site for this detector," he said. "It turns very slowly and it has no atmosphere, so when you look at the horizon it is perfectly sharp. A mountain ridge would act like a knife edge on radiation from stars rising and setting over that horizon. The idea is this: the detector faces the horizon. As an X-ray source goes over the horizon, we detect a signal. Then, very abruptly, it will disappear. If it is a very small, starlike source, it will disappear almost instantly, and we'll know its position with very high precision."

Friedman's enthusiasm for his work is contagious. Like Grote Reber in radio astronomy, Herbert Friedman was alone in the field of X-ray astronomy at first. But now the number of X-ray astronomers has multiplied, and continues to multiply.

At the one hundred and twenty-first meeting of the American Astronomical Society in 1966, astronomers heard

Homer E. Newell of NASA describe the work of Friedman and his colleagues as having produced "some of the most unexpected discoveries and exciting results in space astronomy." Citing the importance of all kinds of astronomical research in the current space program, Newell called for a growing partnership between ground-based astronomers and those in space. "The next decades," he predicted, "could well be the golden age of astronomy."

SELECTED BIBLIOGRAPHY

Armitage, Angus, *William Herschel*, Doubleday and Company, Inc., New York, 1963.

Baumgardt, Carola, editor and translator, *Johannes Kepler, Life and Letters*, Philosophical Library, New York, 1951.

Bolton, Sarah K., *Famous Men of Science* (revised edition), Thomas Y. Crowell Company, New York, 1960.

Brodrick, James, *Galileo*, Harper & Row Publishers, Inc., New York, 1965.

Calder, Nigel, *Radio Astronomy*, Roy Publishers, New York, 1958.

Clerke, Agnes Mary, *The Herschels and Modern Astronomy*, Cassell & Co., London and New York, 1895.

Crowther, J. G., *Six Great Astronomers*, Hamish Hamilton, London, 1961.

de Santillana, Giorgio, *The Crime of Galileo*, University of Chicago Press, 1955.

de Vaucouleurs, Gerard, *Discovery of the Universe*, The Macmillan Company, New York, 1957.

Fermi, Laura, and Bernardini, Gilberto, *Galileo and the Scientific Revolution*, Basic Books, New York, 1961.

Geymonat, Ludovico, *Galileo Galilei* (translated from the Italian by Stillman Drake), McGraw-Hill Book Company, New York, 1965.

Glasstone, Samuel, *Sourcebook on the Space Sciences*, D. Van Nostrand Company, Inc., New York, 1965.

Hyde, Frank W., *Radio Astronomy*, Weidenfeld & Nicholson, Ltd., London, 1962.

Koestler, Arthur, *The Sleepwalkers*, The Macmillan Company, New York, 1959.

Kuhn, Thomas S., *The Copernican Revolution*, Random House, Inc. (Modern Library Paperback), New York, 1959.

Ley, Willy, *Watchers of the Skies*, The Viking Press, New York, 1963.

Lovell, Sir Bernard, *The Exploration of Outer Space*, Harper & Row Publishers, Inc., New York, 1962.

Macpherson, Hector, *Makers of Astronomy*, Oxford University Press, Inc., London, 1933.

Moulton, Forest, and Schifferes, Justus, *The Autobiography of Science* (revised edition), Doubleday and Company, Inc., New York, 1960.

Neal, Harry Edward, *The Telescope*, Simon & Schuster, Inc., Julian Messner Publications, New York, 1958.

Newton, Sir Isaac, *Opticks* (based on the 4th edition, London, 1730), Dover Publications, Inc., New York, 1952.

Page, Thornton and Lou, editors, *Telescopes: How to Make Them and Use Them*, The Macmillan Company, New York, 1966.

Robinson, Thomas Romney, "An Account of the Earl of Rosse's Great Telescope," *Proceedings of the Royal Irish Academy*, Dublin, 1845.

Rosse, William Parsons, Third Earl of, *Scientific Papers*, P. Lund Humphries & Co., London, 1926.

Sidgwick, John B., *William Herschel*, The Macmillan Company, New York, 1954.

Singer, Charles, *A Short History of Scientific Ideas to 1900*, Oxford at the Clarendon Press, London, 1959.

Thiel, Rudolf, *And There Was Light* (translated from the Ger-

man by Richard and Clara Winston), Alfred A. Knopf, Inc.,
New York, 1957.

Thomas, Shirley, *Men of Space*, Chilton Book Company, Philadelphia, 1965.

Wright, Helen, *Explorer of the Universe*, E. P. Dutton & Co.,
Inc., New York, 1966.

INDEX

Accademia del Lincei, 25
Adams, John Couch, 131
Airy, Sir George, 131-132
American Astronomical Society, 232
Ångström, Anders Jonas, 202
angstrom unit, 202
Archimedes, 18-19
Aristotle, 19, 26
Armagh Observatory, Ireland, 125
Armati, Salvino degli, 4
astrology, 43
atomic bombs, 222
August, Carl, 176
Ayscough, Hannah, 62-63

Baade, Walter, 225
Badovere, Jacques, 5
Banks, Sir Joseph, 97
Barrow, Isaac, 59, 69
Barton, Catharine, 67, 79
Bell Telephone Laboratories, 188, 198-199, 207
"big bang" theory, 229

Birr Castle, Ireland, 120, 127, 130, 132-133
Black Death, England, 61, 66
Bode, Johann, 97
Bond, George P., 172
Bowyer, Stuart, 224
Brahe, Tycho, 49-51, 170, 226
Bunsen, Robert, 118
Burnham, Shelbury Wesley, 142
Byram, Edward T., 224-225

Caldwell, O. H., 194
California Institute of Technology, 137, 156, 158
Cambridge University, 65-66, 69, 74
Carnegie, Andrew, 155
Cassegrainian reflector, 175
Cassini, Domenico, 99
Cesi, Prince Federico, 25-26
Chalmers Institute of Technology, 171
Chicago, University of, 152
Chubb, Talbot A., 224
Clark, Alvan, 142, 152

239

color rings, on lenses, 108-109; see also light
Columbus, Christopher, 14
comet, 22; Halley's, 78-79
compound lens, 110
Comte, Auguste, 118
Copernican theory, 44-47
Copernicus, Nicolaus, 11, 48
Corning glass works, 159-160
Cosmic Mystery, The (Kepler), 48, 51
Crab nebula, 199, 226-227
Cygnus A, radio star, 199

Daguerre, Jacques, 171-172
Demisiani, Ionnes, 26
De Motu (Galileo), 19
Dialogue (Galileo), 27-29
Dioptrice (Kepler), 39-40
Dollond, John, 109-110
Dorpat refractor, 115
Drake, Sir Francis, 15
Draper, John William, 171
DuBridge, Lee, 137

earth, gravitation of, 68
electromagnetic spectrum, 201-203
Elizabeth I, England, 15
Euclid, 19
eyeglasses, first, 4

falling bodies, law of, 19-20
Florence, Italy, 14, 19, 31
fluxions, 76, 78
Franklin, Benjamin, 25
Fraunhofer, Franz Xavier, 106
Fraunhofer, Joseph von, 104-

Fraunhofer (*cont.*)
109, 128, 144-145, 171; spectroscope and, 111
Fraunhofer lenses, 107-109, 117
Fraunhofer lines, 111-113, 148
Fraunhofer telescope, 115
frequency, wavelength and, 201
Friedman, Herbert, 212-233; early rocket experiments, 212ff.; with Naval Research Laboratory, 221ff.; Rockoon experiments, 222-223; discovers X-ray galaxies and neutron stars, 228-230; on future of X-ray astronomy, 230-231

galaxies, colliding, 199; X-ray, 226-230
Galilei, Galileo, 7-31, 69; his telescope, 9; discovers moons of Jupiter, 9-11, 25; discovers isochronism, 17-18; and law of falling bodies, 19-20; his studies in mechanics, 21-23; study of moon, 22-25; correspondence with Kepler, 35-36, 48-49
Galilei, Vincenzo, 14-16
Geiger counter, 217, 222-223
George III, England, 86, 96, 98
Giacconi, Riccardo, 223
Grantham school, England, 63-65
gravitation, Newton's law of, 66-68, 78-79
Green Bank, Va., radio astronomy observatory, 205-206

Gregory XIII, Pope, 15
Guinand, Pierre Louis, 107, 114
Gursky, Herbert, 223

Hale, George Ellery, 137-163, 222; spectroheliograph work, 148-150; director of Yerkes Observatory, 154; of Mount Wilson Observatory, 155-158
Hale Telescope, 137-139, 141, 159-163
Halley, Edmund, 75-79
Halley's comet, 78-79
Hamburg Observatory, 177-178, 185
Harvard Observatory, 148-149
helium, discovery of, 145
Herschel, Caroline, 89-90, 93, 96, 98, 103
Herschel, Dietrich, 83, 89
Herschel, Isaac, 83-85
Herschel, Jacob, 83, 86
Herschel, Sir John, 172
Herschel, Mary (Mrs. William Herschel), 99
Herschel, William (Friedrich Wilhelm), 81-103, 115, 126, 131, 139, 171; as musician, 84-86; preoccupation with stars, 90; on telescope power, 91-92; as telescope builder, 97-98; his Observatory House, 98; studies of double stars, nebulae, 101
Hey, J. Stanley, 198, 228
Holden, Edward S., 150
Holmes, Burton, 142

Hooke, Robert, 75
Hooker telescope, Mount Wilson, 157
horoscopes, 51, 53
Hough, George Washington, 143
Huggins, William, 145
Huygens, Christian, 99

Illinois Institute of Technology, 194
International Geophysical Year, 223
Irish famine of 1848, 130

Jansky, Karl, 188-194, 199, 207-208, 212
Janssen, Zacharias, 3
Jodrell Bank radio telescope, 205
Johns Hopkins University, 215, 221
Jupiter, moons of, 9-11, 22, 25, 35

Kefer, Father Xavier, 107
Kenwood Physical Laboratory, 147, 151
Kepler, Heinrich, 40
Kepler, Johannes, 32-56, 59, 67, 69, 170, 226; telescope of, 39; correspondence with Galileo, 48-49
Kepler's laws, 52-53
Kirchhoff, Gustav Robert, 118, 129

Law of Universal Gravitation, Newton's, 66-68, 78-79

lenses, color refraction in, 108-109; Fraunhofer's work with, 107-109; for refracting telescope, 91, 115-116, 150

Leo X, Pope, 43

Leverrier, Urbain Jean-Joseph, 131

"Leviathan" telescope, 120, 127-136

Lick Observatory, 142, 150

light, color and, 67, 73, 108-111; straight-line path of, 34-35; velocity of, 201

Lincei, Accademia del, 25

Lippershey, Hans, 1-5

Lockyer, Norman, 145

Maestlin, Michael, 44

manned space observatory, 230

Maskelyne, Nevil, 94

Massachusetts Institute of Technology, 146, 223

mass and weight, 68

mathematics, astronomy and, 16, 42

Mauritz of Nassau, 3

"Medicean Stars," 12-13

Medici, Cosimo de', 12

Medici, Julian de', 36

Message from the Stars (Galileo), 12, 35

Metius, Jacobus, 3

Milky Way, 101, 188, 195-197, 226; signals from, 188, 195

mirror, in reflecting telescope, 92-93, 116, 126-127

Monte, Guidobaldo del, 19

moon, Galileo's study of, 22-24; photographs of, 171-172; telescope on, 230, 232

Mount Palomar observatory and telescope, 80, 139, 155-157, 160-161, 165-166, 185

Mount Wilson observatory and telescope, 139, 155-157, 196

Munich Academy, 114

National Aeronautics and Space Administration, 209, 214, 217

National Bureau of Standards, 199

National Radio Astronomy Observatory, 205

Naval Research Laboratory, U.S., 212, 217

nebulae, 102, 127, 132, 134-135

Neptune, discovery of, 131

Neuchâtel, Switzerland, lens making in, 107

neutron star, 224, 226

Newell, Homer E., 233

Newton, Sir Isaac, 54, 57-80, 175, 183; grinds lenses, 60; light experiments, 60-61, 67, 73; "apple" story, 67-68; professor at Cambridge, 69-70; builds telescope, 70-71; his "fluxions," 76; his Principia, 77

Nicholas I, Russia, 116

novae, 22, 170; see also super-novae

Noyes, Alfred, 156

On the Revolutions of the Heavenly Spheres (Copernicus), 11

Oppenheimer, J. Robert, 225

Opticks (Newton), 78, 109

Optics (Kepler), 35, 59

Orbiting Astronomical Observatory, 231

Orbiting Solar Observatories, 220-221

"oscillating" theory, 229

Oxmantown, Lord, 122-124

Padua, University of, 21

Palomar Observatory, *see* Mount Palomar observatory and telescope

Paolini, F. A., 223

Parsons, Sir Lawrence, 122, 128

Parsons, William, *see* Rosse, Lord

Parsonstown telescope, 120, 126-136

pendulum, principle of, 17-18

Philosophical Society, Philadelphia, 25

photography, invention of, 171-172; telescope and, 164-187

photomeasurement, 35

Pickering, Edward, 147

Pisa, Italy, 14-15, 19; Leaning Tower of, 20; University of, 19

Pitt, Mary (Mrs. William Herschel), 99

planets, Galileo's study of, 23-25; size and speed of, 45-46

Porta, Giambattista della, 4

Prague, Kepler's and Tycho Brahe's work in, 51-53

Principia (Newton), 77

Pulkovo Observatory, Russia, 116-117

pyrex mirror, 160-163

quadrants, astronomical, 38

quartz mirror, 159

quasars, 208-210, 228-229

radar, 198

radio astronomy, 188-190

radio galaxy, 228

radio signals, from stars, 188, 191, 197, 212-230

radio telescope, 203-204, 206

Reber, Grote, 188-212; builds own "radio ear," 196-197

reflecting telescope, 70-72, 91; Herschel's, 92, 100; Newton's, 72; Schmidt's, 157-158; 60-inch, 155; 100-inch, 155-156; 200-inch, 159-163

refracting telescope, 91, 115-116, 150; *see also* telescope

refraction, law of, 34-35; color fringes and, 108-109

Reuttinger, Susanna, 53

Ricci, Ostilio, 16-17

Robinson, Rev. Thomas Romney, 125-127, 131-132

Rockefeller Foundation, 158-159

rocket telescopes, 212-233

Rockoons, 222-223

Roman Catholic Church, geocentric theory and, 11-12; and Reformation, 41-42

Rose, Dr. Wickliffe, 158

Rosse, Lord (William Parsons), 120-136; builds 6-inch metal mirror and reflecting telescope, 126-130; studies nebulae, 127-132

Rossi, Bruno B., 223

Royal Astronomical Society, 102

Royal Irish Academy, 125

Royal Society of London, 25, 72, 77, 94, 127

Rudolph II, Holy Roman emperor, 43, 51, 53

Rudolphine Tables (Kepler), 54

Sandage, Allan R., 208

"satellite," first use of, 37

Saturn, 99

Scheiner telescope, 40

Schmidt, Bernhard, 164-187; early years, 168-170; makes reflecting mirrors, 173-175; as "windmill engineer," 179; at Hamburg observatory, 180-183; first sky photographs, 183-184

Schmidt, Maarten, 209

Schmidt telescope-camera, 164-187

Schorr, Richard, 177-180, 185

Schwarzschild, Karl, 174-177

Secchi, Angelo, 145

Seven Years' War, 84-85

Siderius Nuncius (Galileo), 12, 35

sky photography, beginnings of, 171; Schmidt telescope-camera and, 164-187

Smith, Rev. Barnabas, 63, 65

solar prominences or flares, 148, 223

solar system, movement of, 102

solar X-rays, 215, 219, 222-224

Somnium (Kepler), 54

Southworth, G. C., 198

space age, 212

Spanish Armada, 15

spectroheliograph, 148-149, 222

spectroscope, 144, 215; first, 111

spectrum, colors of, 109-112, 114

stars, motion of, 101; in nebulae, 127, 130-132

"steady state" theory, 229

Steinheil, Rudolf, 176

Storey, Miss, 63, 66

Struve, Friedrich Georg Wilhelm, 116

sun, X-rays from, 215, 219, 222-224

sunspots, 155-156

supernovae, 170, 199, 209, 226

Taylor, A. H., 198

telescope, Bible and, 26; Galileo's, 9; Hale's, 137-139, 141, 159-163; Herschel's, 100; Kepler's, 39; Lippershey's, 1-5; on moon, 230, 232; Newton's, 70-72; orbiting, 230-232; reflecting, 71-72, 92, 100, 115-116, 155-163; refracting, 91,

telescope (*cont.*)
115-116, 150; Rosse's, 129-136; Scheiner, 40; Schmidt, 157-158; 164-187
telescope-camera, 164-187
Thirty Years' War, 55
Thomas Aquinas, St., 43
Trinity College, Cambridge, 65-66
Trinity College, Dublin, 123

United States Naval Research Laboratory, 212, 217
Uraniborg University, 49
Uranus, 81, 97
Urban VIII, Pope, 28

Venus, 143
Verne, Jules, 136, 142
Vinci, Leonardo da, 14
Volkoff, G. M., 225

von Fraunhofer, *see* Fraunhofer, Joseph von
V-2 rocket, 214

Wallis, John, 78
Watson, Dr. William, 94
wavelength, 201
Weichselberger, Philipp Anton, 106
weight and mass, 68
Wollaston, William Hyde, 112
Woodward, Robert S., 155
Wren, Sir Christopher, 75

X-ray astronomy, 212-230
X-ray star, 228-229

Yerkes, Charles Tyson, 152
Yerkes Observatory, 139, 153-154
Young, L. C., 198

Zwicky, Fritz, 225

ABOUT THE AUTHOR

When Barbara Land was four years old, her grandmother showed her the Big Dipper. She has been an enthusiastic amateur astronomer ever since. To this day she is eagerly anticipating the appearance of Halley's Comet—due by 1986.

While in college, Barbara Land started to work as a newspaper reporter. After her marriage she continued her career, writing radio scripts and magazine articles. Mrs. Land has been a reporter for *The New York Times* and a book editor for *This Week* magazine. In addition, she has taught a graduate course in newswriting at her alma mater, the Columbia University School of Journalism. She is the author of several books for young readers and is the co-author, with her husband, of other books.

Mrs. Land and her husband live in New Rochelle, New York. They have a daughter, who writes poetry, and a son, who is studying to be an astronomer.